FINLEY'S ADVENTURES

98 GOOD TIMES IN NEW ENGLAND AND BEYOND WITH A FAITHFUL COMPANION

SHERRY FENDELL

Copyright © 2024 Sherry Fendell.

All rights reserved. No part of this book may be used or reproduced by any means, graphic, electronic, or mechanical, including photocopying, recording, taping or by any information storage retrieval system without the written permission of the author except in the case of brief quotations embodied in critical articles and reviews.

LifeRich Publishing is a registered trademark of The Reader's Digest Association, Inc.

LifeRich Publishing books may be ordered through booksellers or by contacting:

LifeRich Publishing
1663 Liberty Drive
Bloomington, IN 47403
www.liferichpublishing.com
844-686-9607

Because of the dynamic nature of the Internet, any web addresses or links contained in this book may have changed since publication and may no longer be valid. The views expressed in this work are solely those of the author and do not necessarily reflect the views of the publisher, and the publisher hereby disclaims any responsibility for them.

Any people depicted in stock imagery provided by Getty Images are models, and such images are being used for illustrative purposes only. Certain stock imagery © Getty Images.

ISBN: 978-1-4897-4733-4 (sc)
ISBN: 978-1-4897-4732-7 (hc)
ISBN: 978-1-4897-4734-1 (e)

Print information available on the last page.

LifeRich Publishing rev. date: 03/13/2024

CONTENTS

Acknowledgements vii
Foreword ix
Introduction xi

The Adventures

Meet Finley—May 14, 2020 1
Finley Visits the Sudbury Valley Trustees—May 21, 2020 3
Exploring at Callahan State Park—May 28, 2020 5
Making Friends in the Woods—June 4, 2020 7
A Long Floating Leap and a Big Splash—June 11, 2020 9
A Walk in the King Philip Woods Conservation Land—June 18, 2020 11
The Fields and Pathways of Cow Common—June 25, 2020 13
Climbing Tippling Rock—July 2, 2020 15
A Visit to the Spa—July 9, 2020 17
Finley Meets a Potbelly Pig—July 16, 2020 19
An adventure in the Gray Reservation 23
Finley Enjoys Walking along the Railbed—July 30, 2020 25
Finley Meets Cousin Bo—August 6, 2020 27
A Lake Swim on a Lazy Summer Afternoon—August 13, 2020 29
Visiting Dutton Downs in Sudbury—August 20, 2020 31
A New Toy and a Swim—August 27, 2020 33
Finley Goes to a Secret, Magical Place—September 3, 2020 35
Exploring Wright Woods in Concord—September 10, 2020 37
Hanging Out in the Backyard—September 17, 2020 39
Fresh Finds at Hop Brook—September 24, 2020 41
Visiting Callahan State Park—October 1, 2020 43
Three Days in Maine—October 8, 2020 45
Canoeing on the Sudbury and Concord Rivers—October 15, 2020 47
Three Adventures in Ten Hours—October 22, 2020 49
Finley Revisits Wright Woods in Autumn—October 29, 2020 51
Halloween, 2020 Style—November 5, 2020 53
A Trip to Noon Hill in Medfield—November 12, 2020 55
A Little Boy and a Football—November 19, 2020 57

A Massage Fit for a Dog—November 26, 2020 59
A Visit to Ponyhenge—December 3, 2020 61
Forest Bathing—December 10, 2020 63
Finley Finds Symbols of Peace—December 17, 2020 65
Snow Day—December 24, 2020 67
Finley Discovers Ford's Folly in Framingham—December 31, 2020 69
A Trip to Vermont—January 7, 2021 71
A Visit to Great Brook Farm—January 14, 2021 73
The Pup Turns Two—January 21, 2021 75
A New Equine Friend—January 28, 2021 77
A Romp in the Snow—February 4, 2021 79
A Return Visit to Wright Woods—February 11, 2021 81
First Nor'easter Brightened This Dog's Day—February 18, 2021 83
A Visit to White Pond—February 25, 2021 85
A Return Visit to Danforth Falls—March 4, 2021 87
A Giant Snow Woman—March 11, 2021 89
Visiting Hazel Brook Conservation Land—March 18, 2021 91
A Visit to the Haynes Garrison House—March 25, 2021 93
A Springtime Visit to Wright Woods—April 1, 2021 95
Traveling to Gloucester on Cape Ann—April 8, 2021 97
A Spring Romp at Gates Pond—April 15, 2021 99
A Beaver Dam on Hop Brook—April 22, 2021 101
A Visit to Baiting Brook-Welch Reservation—April 29, 2021 103
A Visit to Trap Falls in Ashby—May 6, 2021 105
On the Ghost Trail and Beyond—May 13, 2021 107
Looking Back on All the Fun—May 20, 2021 109
A visit to Delaney Pond—May 27, 2021 111
Finley and Bo Visit the deCordova Sculpture Park—June 3, 2021 113
Celebrating Prairie's Special Day—June 10, 2021 115
Finley Savors a Sunset and Barks at a Leopard—June 17, 2021 117
Finley Visits the Historic Wayside Inn in Sudbury—June 24, 2021 119
A Visit to Peach Hill and the Nashoba Valley Winery—July 1, 2021 121
Some Previously Unpublished Photos—July 8, 2021 123
A Walk after the Rain—July 22, 2021 125
Hop Brook—July 29, 2021 127
A Lazy Trip down the Sudbury River—August 5, 2021 129
Visiting Dog Beach in Nahant—August 12, 2021 131
Finding Places to Cool Off—August 19, 2021 133

A Visit to Concord—August 26, 2021 135
Finley Enjoys a Visit to Bearly Read Books—September 2, 2021 137
Finley Visits His Favorite Veterinarian—September 9, 2021 139
Finley Swims and Retrieves under a Waterfall—September 16, 2021 141
Chillaxing—September 23, 2021 143
Finley Spends Four Days in Old Cape Cod, Part 1: Cape Cod Bay—September 30, 2021 145
Old Cape Cod, Part 2: Two Ocean Beaches—October 7, 2021 147
Old Cape Cod, Part 3: The Dunes and the Lighthouse—October 14, 2021 149
Making Friends with Courtney—October 21, 2021 151
Visiting Newburyport's Waterfront—October 28, 2021 153
A Surprise for Finley—November 4, 2021 155
Errands around Town—November 11, 2021 157
A Trip to Forty Caves—November 18, 2021 159
Photogenic Finley Wishes You a Happy Thanksgiving—November 25, 2021 161
Stirring Up Friendly Spirits along the Sudbury River—December 2, 2021 163
Skills with a Softball—December 9, 2021 165
Finley Visits Halibut Point State Park—December 23, 2021 167
Finley Savors a Bowser Beer and a Beefy Cigar—December 30, 2021 169
Three Adventures in Concord and Carlisle—January 6, 2022 171
Finley Speaks!—January 13, 2022 173
Finley Teaches Himself an Acrobatic Stick Game—January 20, 2022 175
Finley Visits an Apple Orchard—February 3, 2022 177
Finley Inspects Upper Mill Brook—February 10, 2022 179
Finley Participates in a Game of Mental Stimulation—February 24, 2022 181
Covered Bridges and Great Friends in Vermont—March 17, 2022 183
Making Friends on a Walk along Hop Brook—March 24, 2022 185
Playing in the White Sand at Crane Beach in Ipswich—March 31, 2022 187
A Visit to Singing Beach in Manchester-by-the-Sea—April 7, 2022 189
Having a Ball on Wingaersheek Beach in Gloucester—April 14, 2022 191
A Visit to Rocky Woods and Rocky Narrows—April 21, 2022 193
A Bit of a Misadventure at Elm Bank Reservation—April 28, 2022 195
Visiting Cowassock Woods and Ashland Town Forest—May 5, 2022 197
Visiting Coney Island in Brooklyn, New York—May 12, 2022 199
Additional Images of Finley 201

Epilogue 217
About the Author 218

ACKNOWLEDGEMENTS

I would like to express my deepest gratitude to the following people: Charles Leahy for your poetic book description and your interesting insights into the character of "Master Finley;" Margaret Rice Cross, for your proofreading and your encouragement; Anna Warrock, for penning the foreword section of the book; Eunice Whipple, for assisting with the table of contents and uploading the images; Judy and Adrian Sheldon, for assisting with the book layout; Alexander Fendell and Courtney Whipple, who love Finley with all of their hearts and eagerly looked forward to reading another weekly installment of "Finley's Adventures".

I would also like to thank my family, friends and acquaintances who consistently shared their reactions to the columns and offered their encouragement and support: Linda Fields, Madelon Hope, Dorothy Douthit, Jean Betz and Nina Von Gerichten, Steve Isenberg and Flavio, Claudiana, and Kaio Oliveira.

Finally, I would like to thank the people that Finley and I meet along the way, who were sources of interesting information relevant to the adventure at hand.

I could not have undertaken this journey without you.

FOREWORD

You're about to go on an adventure.

Have you driven past a state park and had a fleeting thought that you might want to get out of the car and take a walk? Do you recall the name of a hike near your home that you always meant to check out? What about taking a day to meander along a lovely stretch of beach on the North Shore of Massachusetts or stay at a mountain inn overlooking Lake Champlain and the Adirondack Mountains of New York?

Sherry Fendell is your guide! After reading these marvelous columns, you will come up with a list, and next weekend you will get outside and go for that walk––for sure!

Sherry's enthusiasm and humor encourage exploration. In these accounts of her rambles, whether near her Sudbury home or farther afield, you learn a bit of history, geology, botany, and mythology. As you vicariously walk through these pages, you may ponder a meaningful quote, as in her April 21, 2022, column. You will understand that right outside your door and just down the highway there are easy daytrips that you can tackle alone or share with friends.

Finley, the ninety-pound yellow English Labrador who accompanies Sherry, says emphatically that we are here to enjoy every moment. His photogenic energy graces each story––with a stick or a ball––and Sherry reports on the meaning behind every soulful gaze and every wag of his thick otter tail. Occasionally, Finley speaks his wisdom directly to us––and it's always, *Have fun!*

Sherry's adventures include her friendships with neighbors and strangers alike, for example, a little boy who asks whether this delightful person sharing her fantastic dog could really be considered a grown-up. Her many unexpected and graceful encounters include the rocks and streams, the flora and fauna. Along with Sherry, you'll be encouraged to stop along a roadside to check out a pond in New Hampshire fronting Mount Monadnock, the second most-summitted mountain in the world––or some other phenomenon of this strange and wonderful life.

Let these fine stories of Sherry and Finley renew your sense of wonder. Who knows what you'll find?

Anna M. Warrock
Somerville, Massachusetts

INTRODUCTION

As I looked back at Finley's first photograph taken in February 2019 when he was eight weeks old, it was evident that he was a handsome, block-headed English Labrador retriever puppy with soulful brown eyes. What the photo didn't show were the large white circles of light that adorned each shoulder; I came to call them his "angel wings," though they bore no resemblance to wings.

In April 2020 when COVID-19 was in full swing and most of us were sheltered, socially distanced, and pandemic cautious, Finley and I were lucky to have access to an abundance of natural areas. We reveled in hiking through the forests, fields, and beaches of New England. I was now masked, even in the great outdoors, as we walked the familiar trails and explored the unknown paths with fun and adventure in mind. Adventures and joie de vivre were the happy results of our explorations.

From May 2020 through May 2022, I authored a weekly newspaper column in the *Sudbury Town Crier* entitled Finley's Adventures. The stories contained descriptions of Finley's behaviors and often contained historical, geological, or geographic references, which acted as a setting for the stories that unfolded. The columns demanded photos of Finley in action, and I included them. Beginning with the third story, I incorporated epigraphs from comedic essayists, transcendentalists, industrialists, poets and songwriters that introduced the latest adventure.

Finley began to be recognized by his readers as he romped through the conservation lands of Sudbury, MA, a town twenty-four miles west of Boston and with a rich colonial history. People spoke of the laughs and smiles that the stories elicited. They talked about being glad to be given the resources that would lead them to having their own adventures with their dogs or children. Some people asked to be posed for photos with Finley to share with family and friends. During the course of those two years, Finley posed in a Vermont phone booth during a snowstorm, in a colonial-era graveyard, and next to a group of rocking horses that he thought were real. He never minded.

Finley is a puppy unlike any other that I have mothered in my thirty-five years of raising yellow Labs. As an example, Finley taught himself to play soccer; he mastered his version of the game, rolling and bumping his soccer ball along through the woods, using his nose and front paws to direct the ball and deftly avoiding all obstacles. It was quite a sight to behold.

In response to reading another adventure, my dear friend Charles Leahy commented, "What I have come to appreciate is that this canine protagonist, while real, has become a fictive character, humanized, and who participates in decision-making, has a heart and a brain, and loves to look out on the world going by."

I have been asked by many of my readers to compile these stories in a book.

Please come along with us for the ride.

Sherry Fendell
November, 2023

Meet Finley

May 14, 2020

The idea for this column came from the poem "Caged Bird", by Maya Angelou.

The poem reflects on the longing for freedom of a bird that finds itself caged, a bird plaintively calling out his deep need to fly fee.

During these long months of relative confinement due to the ravages of COVID-19, I thought that it would be fun for people to read about the adventures of sixteen - month - old Finley, who is a joyful yellow Labrador Retriever pup. He loves to run free in the conservation lands and swim in its streams, always having a blast.

Finley as an eight week-old puppy.

Finley meets and bothers Lulu, the girl next door.

Finley runs with a stick in Maine when he was six months old.

Finley Visits the Sudbury Valley Trustees

May 21, 2020

This week's adventure with Finley takes us to Wolbach Farm in Sudbury, the headquarters of the Sudbury Valley Trustees. SVT is a regional land trust, doing extraordinary work in pursuit of land acquisition, advocacy, and education.

    First, Finley poses in front of a redbud tree at Wolbach Farm. Next, Finley encounters a small waterfall, made fuller by the plentiful spring rains. His leap is made possible by pure muscle. In the last photo, Finley is running through the woods with a big stick in his mouth, on the winding trail of the property—the bigger the stick, the better. I actually think that Finley would prefer sticks to his chow if given the choice!

Finley leaps over a stream.

Finley runs with a stick on the loop trail.

Exploring at Callahan State Park

May 28, 2020

🐾

The beautiful Spring came, and when nature resumes
her loveliness, the human soul is apt to revive also.
—Harriet Ann Jacobs

This week, Finley delighted in the fragrance of wildflowers, and ran through some of the many trails at Callahan State Park, which covers 958 acres, mostly in Framingham and Marlboro. Callahan has nearly a hundred acres of open fields, and there are an additional seventy acres that are under agricultural lease. There is also an especially scenic pond in the park.

Finley's adventures included cavorting in a puddle with another yellow Lab. They had just met. It's marvelous to see that when dogs like each other right away, nothing gets in the way of the two forming an instant friendship.

I took the cloud reflection photo about a month ago before the trees began to leaf out. Here we see Finley surveying the landscape.

Running in the tall grass

Finley wanders through a field of yellow wildflowers at Callahan State Park.

Finley is surveying the trees and fields.

Making Friends in the Woods

June 4, 2020

🐾

Of all of the sights that I love in this world,
and there are plenty—very near the top of the
list is this one: dogs without leashes.
—Mary Oliver

This week, somewhere in the Sudbury woods near the Gray Reservation, fourteen-year old Alex saw Finley, excitedly swimming in the direction of a stick that was hurled into a stream. Although Alex's father was standing close by with the family's small terrier in tow, Alex had eyes only for Finley.

If truth be told, Finley enjoys the thrill of going after sticks, but not necessarily bringing them back. So, in order to continue the game, Alex was forced to enter the stream and retrieve the discarded sticks for himself. Thirty minutes of great fun ensued.

Alex's father stood by, observing and smiling at the classic boy–super-pup duo.

I suggested that he might want to call Lab Rescue and inquire about adding another dog to his household.

After a while, Alex told me that he wanted to see Finley again. How is that for asking what you want?

We have a date on Saturday morning.

Finley makes some mulch

A Long Floating Leap and a Big Splash

June 11, 2020

The poet Robert Bly metaphorically speaks of leaping not so much as exercise, but more as freeing your mind to the possibilities.

This week, we explored the Haynes Meadow Conservation land, a thirty-seven-acre parcel, purchased by the town in 1986 with the help of state funds. We walked by picturesque wet meadows and along a glacial esker. The latter is defined as "a long, narrow winding ridge, composed of stratified sand and gravel deposited in the last glacial period 10,000 years ago."

Finley, as a sixteen-month-old Labrador retriever, has begun to leap from embankments in order to get to his beloved sticks even faster. By swimming every day throughout the year, he has become a strong boy and a fabulous swimmer. In one of these photos, you can see him swimming hard against the current. I believe that Finley could easily be trained to become a water-rescue dog.

Leap well, Finley.

Leap well.

Finley is in a hurry to retrieve the stick in the water.

Finley makes a big splash as he jumps in the water.

Finley swims against the current.

A Walk in the King Philip Woods Conservation Land

June 18, 2020

🐾

At the end of heaven's rainbow, there's
a treasure that I found.
—Greenwolfe

This week Finley and I rounded the pond in the King Philip Woods Conservation Land in Sudbury. This was our second visit, only to be surprised that we were its only visitors, on both occasions. This made for an especially peaceful walk.

This conservation land was named after King Philip's War, a significant war in southern New England, which lasted from June 1675 to August 1676. The war acquired its name from Metacomet, who was called King Philip by the English colonial authorities, and was the second son of Massasoit, the hereditary leader (*sachem*) who had entered into a peace treaty with leaders of the Plymouth Colony in 1621. In this war, an alliance of Native American (Indian) tribes attempted to eliminate all of the immigrant colonial residents so that the Native Americans could regain control of their former lands and put an end to the poor treatment by the English colonial authorities and, in some cases, settlers. The "Sudbury fight" played a major role in causing the turning point in the war.

Soon after Finley ran into the pond, he began to grapple with an object at his feet. He brought up a deflated volleyball that may have been submerged for years. The muddy ball blocked his face as he came running out the pond. His newly found ability to do this stunned me.

About halfway around the pond, Finley came upon an old tire. He began to rip the rubber away from the rim, and would have completed the job, had I not called him to continue on our walk.

Last but not least, Finley saw a Pride mask hanging from a tree branch. Although he never attended a Pride parade, 2020 marks the fiftieth anniversary of gay pride celebrations, he was happy to play with his third find of the day. As they say, "Pride marches on!"

Finley found a tire in the water of the woods of King Philip Woods Conservation Land.

The Fields and Pathways of Cow Common

June 25, 2020

🐾

May all your weeds be wildflowers.
—sign posted on a tree at the Wayland Community Gardens

On a hot morning early this week, Finley and I explored the Cow Common Conservation Area in Wayland. Consisting of large open fields, the area's fresh smells, rabbits, and wildflowers practically turned him into a whirling dervish. He didn't know where to go first.

Off the path, among a pretty section of buttercups, stood a raised wooden post. It called for a game. Would Finley fetch a stick on the other side of the post, race back toward me, and jump over the post (with encouragement) for his grand finale?

Goodness, no. Under the post he went. Smart boy.

Heading down the path, we soon came upon a pink ribbon with a sign asking us to detour through the woods. We didn't know where the path would lead us. The cordoned-off grassland was created by the Wayland Conservation Department to protect nesting bobolinks, a federally protected bird that migrates from South America. Many of the fields at Cow Common and a sister field, Heard Farm, are part of Wayland's Habitat Management Program.

Leaving the woods, we ran right into the Wayland Community Gardens. Because the gardens are federally funded, residents of other cities and towns can farm there as well.

By this time, Finley was getting a little tired and lay down to rest while I talked to Kathy from Natick, who called herself a "scruffy farmer." She told me that her neighbor's farm plot was always so neat that she figured that the pathways between the vegetables was vacuumed every night after she left.

It was now 9:30 a.m., eighty degrees, and time to head home.

Finley hangs out at the Wayland Community Gardens.

Finley running a top speed at Cow Common in Wayland.

Finley stops to smell the wildflowers at Cow Common in Wayland.

Will Finley approaches a fence as he runs with a stick in his mouth.

Climbing Tippling Rock

July 2, 2020

🐾

My feet touch earth
My face touches sky
I run through the morning
I am alive in this world.
—Kate Coombs

Tippling Rock is located in the Boy Scouts Nobscot Reservation in Sudbury. It is easy to get lost once you leave the main paths, since there are many unmarked side trails. Former logging roads crisscross the reserve.

As you may know, glaciers radically transformed our landscape during the last ice age, (12,000–18,000 years ago) leaving distinct features. One of them is a glacial erratic, which is a non-native glacially deposed rock. Finley successfully climbed one, in order to "rescue" a stick. Whenever he succeeds in retrieving a stick in a difficult location, he holds his tail higher than usual and looks directly at me to receive a resounding verbal approval for his prowess.

Continuing down the path, we saw a vernal pool ahead. A vernal pool is a shallow seasonal pool that fills each spring with rain and snow melt, and then dries up in the heat of the summer. Finley had a grand time cooling off here and I delighted in the sounds of the birds and the sounds of this seventeen-month-old ray of sunshine splashing around.

After another fifteen minutes of walking, we took another side trail that led us directly up to Tippling Rock. It was a very short but steep scramble to the top. Tippling Rock mostly stands out above the trees and affords a great view of downtown Boston, about thirty miles away. From there, you can see the Prudential and John Hancock buildings on the horizon. Supposedly, the two skyscrapers, One Dalton Place and Millennium Tower can be seen on a clear day, but I've never been able to see them.

It was a soft breezy morning, and I was thankful to share another adventure with Finley.

Finley is king of the hill atop Tippling Rock.

A Visit to the Spa

July 9, 2020

🐾

As soap is to the body, so laughter is to the soul.
—Jewish proverb

This is what happens when Finley explores his world. You can see that he splits into a part-black and part-yellow Labrador retriever. The poison hemlock plant that's to his side is one of deadliest plants in North America. Socrates drank a potion of this plant's cousin to end his life. I had always thought that the plant was Queen Anne's lace (wild carrot), which is a wild edible plant. To confuse them would certainly lead to an untimely death. In case you're wondering, the main difference between the two is that poison hemlock has a smooth stem and Queen Anne's lace has a hairy one.

When Finley needs a bath, I have always put him in the bathtub, much to his chagrin. About a month or so ago, I managed to get him into the tub and lather him up. All of a sudden, he leaped out of the tub, knocked me down, and ran out of the room. I landed hard on my tailbone. It was hard to sit down for about three weeks.

Now it was time to let the professionals take over. I took Finley to the recommended Pink Dog Spa in Sudbury, where I received special permission to watch him from a distance and take a couple of pictures.

After his bath, Finley was given a bandana for being a good boy. Since I found the look not quite right for my beastie, I gave it to Lulu, the blond golden retriever next door.

Later on, Finley, psychologically exhausted, rested in the broadleaf weeds that constitute our grass. Thirty-five years ago, I read that the incidence of cancer among dogs was 400 percent higher if herbicide treatments were used to prevent crabgrass and broadleaf weeds on lawns.

I figured that as long as my "lawn" was green, that was good enough for me.

Dirty Finley sitting in front of a stand of Poison Hemlock.

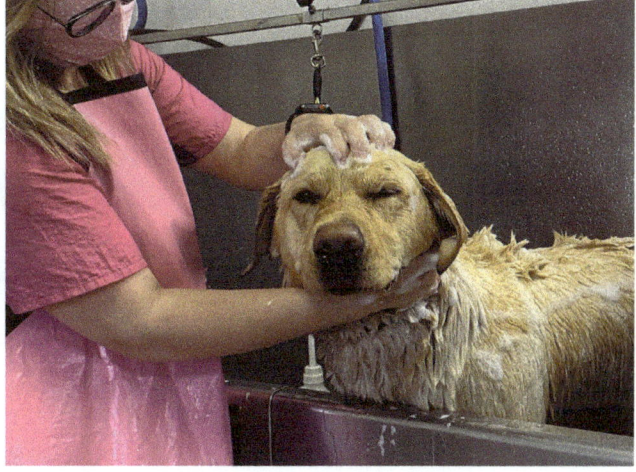

Finley during his first professional bath

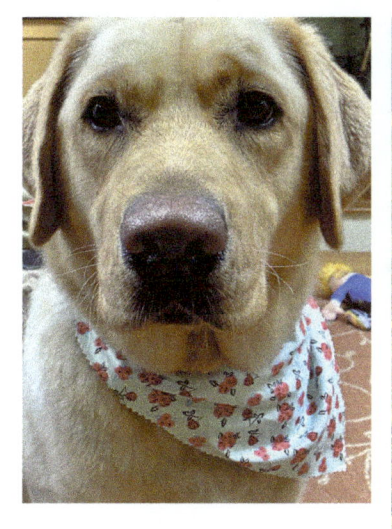

Finley receives a bandanna as a present after his bath.

Finley lounges on his lawn after his bath.

Finley Meets a Potbelly Pig

July 16, 2020

I want a pig. I want a pig on a leash. A baby pig on a leash.
—Kesha

Evan grew up on a farm in Germany and loved pigs, best of all. We met as he was driving by in his painter's truck. He stopped to admire Finley and wanted to know more about him. I regaled him with a Finley story, and he soon told me about Sgt. Schultz, his pot belly pig, a pet that also had some interesting stories. Idea: "Could Finley meet the sergeant and share a little time with him?" Evan readily agreed, and we arranged a date.

At first, Finley stared at the strange being before him, assessing its risk. Then Finley dropped down into a play bow position, but the pig didn't accommodate him.

I asked Evan about the origin of his pet's name. Sgt. Schultz was a character in the 1960s TV series, *Hogan's Heroes*. Evan said that the sergeant was "slow, lumbering, and peaceful," just like his pig. Schultz is a three-year old five-point (five points of white) American potbelly pig, weighing 180 pounds. (Potbelly pigs cannot exceed two hundred pounds or the nomenclature will change.) Schultz likes to eat tomatoes, apples, and weeds, and is always hungry. When Evan said that "Schultz loves balsamic dressing with his lettuce," I thought that he was kidding. He wasn't.

He went on to say that prey animals, such as pigs, do not like to be lifted from the ground. When Schultz was twelve weeks old and living in the house, he loudly screamed whenever he was carried up and down the stairs in order to go out and do his business. One day, Schultz incurred his neighbor's wrath. Considered to be "nuisance livestock," Schultz was in danger of being removed from his home. Five hundred signatures were needed by the authorities to stay a potential order. Evan quickly started an online petition and amassed fifteen hundred signatures from sympathetic people living in different parts of the country. The day was won. Schultz became a famous celebrity in Hudson, and was prominently featured in newspapers in a quite a few local towns.

Schultz grew fast and, one sad day, tripped and fell down the stairs, losing the vision in one eye. Now it was time to live outside. He needed to be protected, so his loving parent built a pigpen for him, with layers of straw to keep him comfortable. Schultz now spends his days listening to country music while gorging on weeds and whatnot.

Meanwhile, Finley continued to run around in happy circles, trying to entice his new friend to play, while Schultz looked on, not once turning his back to the crazy dog, until he'd had enough.

"Perhaps the two boys could wear bandannas the next time they get together?" I asked.

Evan just laughed and said, "He would need a *huge* handkerchief. He is kinda thick around the gills."

Sgt. Schultz is a potbelly pig who lives in Hudson.   **I want a biscuit too!**

Finley seems to wonder, *What is this creature?*

Finley runs toward Sgt. Schultz to invite him to play.

Sgt. Schultz has had enough of Finley for today.

An adventure in the Gray Reservation

July 23, 2020

🐾

The average dog has about 100 different facial expressions. Most of them depend on the movement of his ears, which can be extremely expressive. That's no wonder, since there are a dozen separate muscles that control a dog's ear movements.
—*Dog Fancy*

Along with adjacent conservation lands, the Gray Reservation provides an extraordinary outdoor collection of geologic features, carved by the last glacier over ten thousand years ago. A self-guided glacial features walk, with a scannable QR code or map, describes features of the land and processes that affected it.

Finley loves rambling along these gorgeous trails that take us through white pine and mixed oak woods, past flood plain marshes, and across streams. He enjoys smelling the wildflowers that are abundant in late spring and early summer.

Finley is posing in front of a fireplace and chimney, all that's left of a cabin owned by Stephen and Marjorie Gray. The Gray family created a pond by damming the steam that flows through the property to Hop Brook, a major tributary of the Sudbury River. Ice skating on the pond was followed by dance parties and gatherings around the fireplace at the Grays' cabin in the woods. I can picture all on this fun taking place on a cold winter's day, so many years ago.

Whenever Finley sees a body of water, he goes straight for it and jumps in, no matter the season. Finley jumped into a section of concentrated foam below a ten foot-high waterfall that exited a pond. I always thought that the foam was an example of environmental pollution, and so, I would keep Finley out of this water. This time, he escaped my grip on his collar and dashed toward the foamy stream. I was wrong about the origins of the foam, though, because it is actually the result of natural processes formed when the physical characteristics of the water are altered by the presence of organic materials in the water.

Stephen Gray had died by the time his wife made a gift of their land to the Sudbury Valley Trustees in 1976, for permanent protection as a bird and wildlife sanctuary.

Finley is descending a glacial erratic in Gray Reservation.

Finley poses in front of the chimney that is all that remains of the Gray's cabin in the Gray Reservation.

Finley Enjoys Walking along the Railbed

July 30, 2020

🐾

**Dwell in possibilities.
—Emily Dickinson**

Finley and I and five generations of yellow Labs have spent a great many happy hours walking along the MBTA railbed, which runs for 8.9 miles from Sudbury to Hudson. He thrills to run down to Dudley Brook from a small RR bridge, where he swims and practices his fetching skills. This little brook empties into Hop Brook, then the Sudbury River, the Concord River, the Merrimack River, and finally the Atlantic Ocean. In one of the photos, you can see Finley playing by an old RR signaling structure, which was installed for safety reasons. When I first laid eyes on it in 1978, I began to call it the Monster since it reminded me of a description of an invading Martian that I'd heard in the 1938 Orson Wells radio production of *War of the Worlds*.

Located in the heart of Sudbury, the railbed provides a lovely green space for walking, running, and snowshoeing etc. In 2015, Eversource, the local power company, proposed building 110-foot steel towers, carrying transmission lines, along the entire 8.9-mile right-of-way, in order to meet the supposed electricity demands of their customers. The project involved the clear-cutting of an eighty-two-foot-wide swath (the size of a blue whale) along the railbed. That would cause irreparable damage to our residential neighborhoods, increase our health risks, and harm five continuous conservation lands making up the Hop Brook watershed, including the protected species that live there.

In early 2016, Protect Sudbury, a grassroots group of private citizens, was formed to oppose this project. Broad-based community support came as a result of multiple informative meetings being held to educate residents about what was at stake, should the project go forward. Stopping the Eversource project also became the official position of the town plan to apply herbicides for vegetation management, and the emission of radiation from the high-voltage power lines, were seen as very important objections to the project. In 2016, the herbicide glyphosate was designated by the WHO's cancer agency as a probable carcinogen. We now know, four and a half years later, that glyphosate causes a rare form of blood cancer, called non-Hodgkin's lymphoma. The spray from this toxic chemical would seep into nearby wells, thus adversely affecting our drinking water.

It has been determined that the need for additional electricity has decreased in the last few years.

Thus, the Eversource proposal is not only unnecessary, but more to the point, deeply harmful to all living things.

One of the great paradoxes of psychology states that, "presented with signs that we have made a mistake, we very often choose to discard the evidence and dig in on our prior beliefs." The same can be said for many corporations. Often they retreat even further into their certainties.

The truth is that they really do know fact from fiction.

The Monster

Finley is swimming by the culvert in Dudley Brook.

Finley Meets Cousin Bo

August 6, 2020

🐾

**Laughter is carbonated holiness.
–Ann Lamont**

There's a story, a wonderful one, that uses fly-fishing as its metaphor for life: *A River Runs through It*. But to a certain breed of dog owner, the more apt metaphor is 'A Lab runs through it.' For some, myself included, the Lab in question, will undoubtedly be a yellow Lab. Often, yellow Labs have a coat that is a gorgeous medley of yellow, beige, and white, especially photogenic in the golden light of early morning and late afternoon. Finley, though, has a tiny patch of black on his front side, about the size of a half-dime. Perhaps this is the result of having a black Lab ancestor.

You've been treated to Finley's adventures for a while. My first yellow Lab was Max, born in 1991. On a walk at Callahan State Park with Max, still a puppy, I met Pippa and David who parented a young yellow Lab named Rafter. Max and Rafter hit it off and became soulmates, in the best canine sense of the term.

Whenever Pippa and David (who for the last fifteen years have lived in Westport, Connecticut) have the chance to visit Sudbury, they pay homage to those boys, visiting my pet cementery, located in the quiet of the backwoods.

Finley and Bo meet for the first time.

Bo is totally knackered out and is resting under Amigo.

A Lake Swim on a Lazy Summer Afternoon

August 13, 2020

🐾

It's hot, you know. I can't really stand summer. I prefer to
go out swimming. I think I'll wanna go swimming forever.
—Janelle J. (affirmed by Finley)

Finley and I were delighted to accept an invitation to go swimming in crystal-clear Stiles Lake, which is located in Spencer, about forty-five miles west of Boston, and only one of eighteen lakes in the area.

Of course, Finley jumped out of the car when we arrived, and made a mad dash to the lake about fifty yards away. He jumped in with such force that the splash he made rose over four feet. He doesn't seem to be bothered by belly flops.

In 1863, the industrial might of the country was located in the New England area where hundreds of mills, located in the area's countless streams and rivers, were busily producing a variety of goods for the Union Army. Stiles Lake was central to washing the woolens that were produced in a nearby mill.

In the 1950s, my friend's parents who lived in inland Worcester, bought a house on this four-hundred-acre lake, as did other Worcester residents, many of whom suffered through the long, hot city summers. Today, 70 percent of those living on the lake are year-round residents.

Finley swam and retrieved for five hours, only coming out of the water to shake himself off and ask for treats. I don't think that he really needed an energy boost, because he would have had the energy anyway.

I wanted to paddle my friends' extra kayak, and Finley, having never seen a kayak before, decided to swim along by my side. We were very close to shore. I stopped to take a picture of him as he attempted to jump into the kayak with me. I only wished that I had a larger hull to accommodate him, but in trying to hoist him up into the boat, we likely would have capsized.

A while later, Finley found a floating white object on the other side of the dock. I always thought that it was called a bumper. On the chance that the object had a different name, I sent a photo of it to a friend who lives on a little island off the coast of Abaco in the Bahamas. Of course, a boat is needed there for transporting generators and every other kind of thing. In any case, she informed me that the white object was called a boat fender.

Soon the humans relaxed, sharing good conversation, each partaking in a glass of sauvignon blanc, while Finley drank water from gorgeous Stiles Lake.

Just keep swimming Finley

Finley is attempting to get into my kayak.

Finley is peacefully swimming in Stiles Lake.

Finley is shaking off after retrieving a boat fender.

Visiting Dutton Downs in Sudbury

August 20, 2020

🐾

No philosophers so thoroughly comprehend
us as dogs and horses.
—Herman Melville

Dutton Downs is a lovely ten-acre horse farm that houses fourteen horses, and has been in existence since 1983.

When Finley and I came by for a visit, owners Dottie and Paul Bisson assured me that it was okay for Finley to run around with the horses because they would not at all be threatened by him. Finley was fearless when he met Jazz, the first horse he encountered. He soon spotted the horse's blue ball and ran off with it. Finally, I captured it, threw it back in Jazz's direction, and drew Finley onto the next paddock, which belonged to Logan. Logan is a paint, a breed of horse, often confused with a pinto, which is only defined by its colors.

Dogs and horses are known to rapidly mirror the expression on each other's faces, known as "rapid facial mimicry." I observed this happening with Logan and Finley. After another friendly greeting took place, Logan whinnied, scaring Finley to such an extent that he bolted from the scene, trying to squeeze under a closed gate.

By the way, Logan's orange boots worn to keep the biting flies away, are called Shoofly Leggins.

Twelve of the farm's horses are boarded by owners who take them out riding in nearby conservation lands.

Prairie and Jake belong to Dottie and Paul and are very dear to them. Prairie is a friendly and loving Sioux Indian horse. These type of horses became an important part of Sioux society because the Sioux were nomadic. They moved their villages to places where they had good grass and water for their horses and nearby bison herds. Additionally, the Sioux brought their horses into their tepees at night for safety and mutual comfort.

Jakie is a pony that loved to play a game of Dump the Kid. Dottie explained that ponies are generally much smarter than horses. If a gate were to be left open, Jake would leave his paddock to feast on the fresh, open grass. "He always has one eyeball on the gate." On the other hand, horses would generally just stay put.

Jakie is also a forgiving pony. When a pit bull ripped his nose open last year, he just stood there in shock, but continued to befriend dogs.

After spending a mostly happy hour with the horses from Dutton Downs, and kicking up some dust in the process, Finley was ready to go home for a good hose-down and nap on this very hot and humid August day.

PS. There is an absolutely wonderful story on inter species friendship, meant for adults and children. The book is entitled *Owen and Mzee* by Hatcoff and Hatcoff.

Running around with a horse's toy

Prairie is on the left and Jakie is on the right

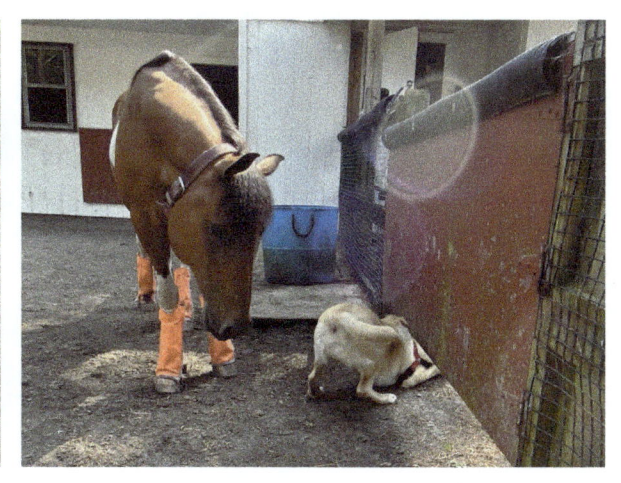

Logan whinnied and Finley got scared.

A New Toy and a Swim

August 27, 2020

It is bad to suppress laughter. It goes back
down and spreads to your hips.
—Fred Allen

We have arrived, orange toy in hand, for Finley's swim. He swims hard, plowing forward like a little Jeep in the clear waters of the Sudbury River. He has had to forgo retrieving and shedding sticks for a while because he lacerated his esophageal tract with a sharp piece of stick that he swallowed. He is excited. Oh for joy, a new toy!

Fresh, clean water is at a premium these days with our continued drought. Our rainfall now measures six inches below average, so Finley's swim in steadily moving water was good for him.

Since Mt. Misery is not a mountain (elevation 284 feet) nor miserable, how did such a lovely place get such a dreary name? There are a couple of local legends that speak to this question. In one, a pair of yoked oxen wandered away from a nearby farm in the late eighteenth century and got stuck on a tree, with the yoke preventing them from moving forward. They ended up dying there. The second legend spoke of sheep that grazed in the area, dying after tumbling over a rocky outcrop. In any case, Mt. Misery has had its name for at least a couple of centuries.

Finley, my friend, and I walked (or ran, as the case may be) along a loop trail for quite some time. When we finally returned to the parking lot, my friend realized that she'd lost her car key somewhere on the trail, necessitating a redo of our original walk. Luckily, she found her key halfway through the second loop. We were a little tired by then.

When Finley and I returned home, he spread out on his favorite chair, and fell asleep next to his dinosaur. It warranted a photograph.

Finley is sleeping peacefully.

Finley Goes to a Secret, Magical Place

September 3, 2020

🐾

**If you stay here you become lost. And no-one can find you.
—Ally Condie**

It is a cool morning in late August, offering just a hint of autumn. Finley seems happier than usual, if that is even possible.

As you know by now, Finley is not keen on summer weather, because he gets very hot in it. This is because, as a Labrador Retriever, he has a short coat that is especially dense and a warm undercoat, both of which together are called a double coat. A warm undercoat allows Labs to keep warm, while swimming in icy water. Labs were first found by British sailors in Labrador and across the straights to Newfoundland, in the early years of the nineteenth century. Swimming in these cold waters, Labs helped fishermen retrieve the fish that fell out of their nets. Because Labs have soft mouths, they never punctured the skin of the fish when they swam back to their masters' boats.

On our forty-five-minute walk to our secret place, we came across a river brimming with a plant called purple loosestrife. Finley hurled himself into the water, landing close to a thicket of it. Although the scenery spreading out before us was very attractive, purple loosestrife cannot be said to grace our wetlands. In fact, it is a highly invasive species, growing rapidly and crowding out our native plants. Originating in Eurasia, purple loosestrife is a plant named by Greek and Roman authors in honor of Lysimachus, the Greek king, and his successful efforts to 'loose' strife, that is, end strife.

Finley noisily poked around the plant, soon leaving it behind. We continued on our walk until we were there. We dropped down about five feet from the little trail that led us here. Finley continued to run around and explore while I sat down on a spot of green, consciously emptying my mind from the world of my many thoughts, slowly breathing in and out, in order to be here now.

Finley and I return to this place often, our aims being different, but both of us loving it just the same.

Can you guess where we are? Hint: It is somewhere in Sudbury.

PS. *Be Here Now* was the best-selling book, written by Baba Ram Dass, an American spiritual teacher and author who helped popularize Eastern spirituality and yoga to the baby boomers in the West.

Finley is enjoying the water's edge near the purple loosestrife.

Our special place

Exploring Wright Woods in Concord

September 10, 2020

In all my rambles I have seen no landscape
which can make me forget Fairhaven
—Henry David Thoreau

I printed a map of Wright Woods, which sits within two thousand acres of protected space in Concord and promised a new adventure for Finley and me. The 3.6-mile perimeter trail would take us past the historic stone boathouse located on the north side of Fairhaven Bay, a lake within the Sudbury River. The perimeter trail was boldly marked on the map so I was not concerned about us losing our way. After about ten minutes of walking, Finley and I came upon an unmarked crossroads, both paths being wide and confusedly veering off in a similar direction. Finley looked at me with a question in his eyes. *Hmmm.*

I said to him, "Let's go," and he chose the path. His guess was as good as mine. Soon enough we encountered another questionable unmarked crossroads. I realized that we didn't want to follow in the footsteps of old Charlie on the MTA. "Well, did he ever return? No he never returned, and his fate is still unlearned."

We found our way back to the parking lot, telling a hiker of our plan and asking for better directions. As it turned out, she was also heading out to hike the loop trail, and invited us to join her. She remarked about finding two other sets of hikers being lost in these woods as well. Though not a dog person, she delighted in Finley's antics and wanted to know all about him. After we spent about thirty minutes on the trail, we arrived at the historic stone boathouse on the north side of Fairhaven Bay. There are hills around the bay, specifically Fairhaven Hill, where Thoreau spent much time recording impressions in his journal, written in the fall of 1850.

"Some distant angle in the sun where a lofty and dense pine wood ... meets a hill covered with shrub oaks, affects me singularly, reinspiring me with all the dreams of my youth. It is a place far away, yet actual."

Because the landscape of that time has many fewer trees than it does today, Thoreau could see many more landmarks than we could see from the same location. It is interesting to note that he accidentally set fire to the woods near the bay in April of 1844. Thoreau lived in his cabin at Walden Pond from 1845 into 1847, an easy walk from the boathouse.

My new friend and Finley and I reached the end of our hike. We all had a wonderful time together and decided to walk the loop again soon.

Finley looks at the historic stone boathouse on Walden Pond.

Finley enjoying Fairhaven Bay.

Hanging Out in the Backyard

September 17, 2020

🐾

The average dog has a mind equivalent to a human 2–3 year old. We recognize that and treat them as if they were human toddlers who need and deserve our care.
—Dr. Stanley Coren, psychologist and dog expert

Finley is in the morning of his days. Although at twenty months he is still considered a puppy, he has amassed quite a number of people who love him, either because they met him or from reading about the way he experiences life. My four-legged friend and I have a very special relationship. I like that he keeps me on a schedule. For example, his morning routine is as follows:

    7:00—first walk of the day
    7:15–8:30—breakfast and a nap
    8:35–10:00—walk in the woods and swim, often with mud included (My friend Adrian once quipped, "Dirty = happy in Lab language")
    10:15–10:30—hose-down and towel-dry
    10:30-Noon—nap

On this particular Sunday morning, we didn't venture out for our usual walk. Instead we hung out in the quiet of our backyard. I set up Finley's new pool so that he could splash around on a day that was fast becoming hotter. He never had a personal pool before and enjoyed it immensely. During the afternoon he took turns playing with an old soccer ball and a new ball, which was called a "wiggle-giggle." The laughing sounds enticed him to run on the grass and through the woods at top speed, pushing the ball forward with his nose and front paws. After about thirty minutes of this highly energetic play, Finley collapsed. Soon he tuned into the sound of a plane as it moved its way across the open sky. I had never seen this particular focused behavior before in any other of my past Labs.

After dinner, Finley switched to retrieving sticks, settling down with them and making mulch for my flowerbeds. By 9:00 p.m., we began to hear the howls of a pack of coyotes. It was eerily wonderful to listen to this chorus. Mars was prominent overhead. It is bright and red now. By late September Mars will match Jupiter in brilliance, one and a third times brighter. The Earth will pass between Mars and the Sun in October for a month or so, centering around mid-October.

The day was now complete. I owe a lot to Finley.

Loves the pool

Finley emerges from the hydrangeas with his ball.

Looking down...

Fresh Finds at Hop Brook

September 24, 2020

Labs rank among the top 10 most intelligent breed of dog on the planet. Breed intelligence is based on obedience and working intelligence and ranks Labs as the 7th highest breed on the canine intelligence scale.

—Stanley Coren

To answer your pressing question, Border Collies are recognized as the most intelligent breed. Known as America's hunting dog, the Lab is one of the best picks for a duck-hunting companion. Labs are friendly toward humans, even toward ducks. I've read that when tracking a downed bird, they smile the whole way through!

Finley also retrieved a duck last week, but a hunter had nothing to do with it. We had just crossed a bridge in the Hop Brook watershed when I spotted a yellow object bobbing along in the water. As it got closer, I could see that it was a rubber duckie. Finley's command for retrieving is "Go get." He hurled himself into the water and retrieved the "cute and yellow and chubby" duck. It was probable that a child had lost or released it somewhere upstream. Maybe the child even sang part of the rubber duckie song as it floated away?

"Rubber duckie, joy of joys. when I squeeze you, you make noise. Rubber duckie, you're my very best friend."

The Hop Brook area was the first conservation tract that I explored over thirty years ago when I parented my first yellow Lab. I know its every path, having walked or cross-country skied it well over a hundred times. About a week prior to finding the rubber duck, I decided to leave the path that Finley and I were taking that morning, and bushwhack through the woods. I knew that in ten to fifteen minutes we would eventually find the trail again.

Finley tore through the woods and suddenly stopped, having found an empty tepee. It was a partially constructed shelter seemingly made for those who desired the peace and quiet of nature, understandable, especially given these difficult times. We made our way back to the tepee a few days later and were taken aback by another surprise, for in the distance I could see figures stirring in sleeping bags. "Stay" was my strong command to Finley, as I grabbed his collar, just to be certain that he would not bolt ahead. Finley started to bark and then two teenagers shot straight up into a sitting position. They saw him and called out to him, with arms outstretched. I quickly released him. Within ten seconds he was exploring their shelter and giving them a few good morning kisses. They laughed. I quickly apologized for our intrusion and literally ran off as quickly as possible in the direction of the trail. Whew! That event was something to remember.

Stick with Finley.

Finley finds a tepee.

Visiting Callahan State Park

October 1, 2020

🐾

As long as one lives, one can learn.
—Ruth Bader Ginsberg

I grew up twelve blocks away from Ruth Bader Ginsberg's hoose and attended her district school, James Madison High School in Brooklyn, New York. It was an ordinary school, yet it produced a Supreme Court justice, six Nobel laureates and three senators. In those days, the great majority of us didn't have dogs, only hamsters, gerbils and goldfish.

On this particular warm and breezy morning in late September, we were inspired to go to Callahan State Park to enjoy its wide-open spaces and undulating pathways. What was immediately apparent as we began our walk were the remarkable smells of autumn. Finley and I set off, soon leaving the main path to investigate a red baler that we saw in the distance. It was nicely framed by a beautiful blue sky and mowed corn stalks.

Tommy Hanson, fifth generation farmer/owner of Hanson's Farm in north Framingham, leases sixty-four acres of parkland to grow corn, pumpkins and winter squash. He told me that if he doesn't farm the land for just two years, it would revert back to meadows and then to second-growth forest.

After Finley ran around the baler for a few minutes, he and I continued walking along the narrow path, lined with spent corn stalks. Both sweet corn and grain corn are grown in these fields. The grain corn is used primarily by the Brazilian community who cook the corn to include in their tasty dishes. The local Brazilian population is the second largest in the country, with Miami being the largest.

Finley galloped ahead, prompted by the bales of hay that he spotted. The warm breezes carried the unforgettable smell of hay drying in the sunshine. Finley spent some happy time sniffing away, and so did I!

As is his way, Finley soon ran to close-by Eagle Pond to enjoy a morning swim. The many kinds of trees reflected in the pond caught my eye. It was a lovely sight.

The next day we returned to the park, hoping for a repeat experience. Alas, it was not to be. The breezes were absent, along with the penetrating power of fall.

PS. If you are looking for a "big sky" sunset, view it from the earthen dam path, 3–4 minutes from the parking lot. Take your first left off the main path.

Finley sniffs a bale of hay.

Playing with his water toy

Three Days in Maine

October 8, 2020

🐾

Live in the sunshine, swim in the sea, drink in the wild air.
—Ralph Waldo Emerson

Finley and I drove up to Goose Rocks Beach, Maine for what promised to be a three-day adventure of beach and ocean exploration. We stayed with old friends who rented a house on this broad sand beach. Bo at five months, is Finley's cousin and good friend. He bounded out of the house to greet Finley as we arrived. The two remained inseparable for our entire stay. There is a cute poster of a dog strenuously wiggling his rear. The caption reads: "Wiggle-Butt." This describes Bo exactly. Having never seen this adorable behavior before, I was completely captured by it.

Goose Rocks Beach stretches for five miles, including a scenic portion of fine white sand. The surf is gentle and the water is relatively warm. Although it is a public beach, there are unfortunately few parking spaces. The beach overlooks distant Goose Rocks and Timber Island, the latter accessible at low tide.

During the day and into the early evening, Finley and Bo ran up and down the beach and in and out of the water. During one particular morning we experienced gale-force winds (sustained winds of 39–54 mph). As we walked along the shore, Finley spotted a medium-sized white ball about a hundred yards out. It was an anchored float. He swam out to retrieve it and would not give up trying to bring his prize back to the beach. Even as I called out, "Liver treats!" and anything else that might entice him to let go of his ball and swim back to shore, he didn't listen. Perhaps he honestly didn't hear me calling out to him above the wind. Not likely. I was readying to strip down and swim out to "retrieve" him, when possibly sensing my frustration, he began to swim back, shaking all over me upon his return!

The next day my friend Pippa consulted a tide chart to determine the time for the next low tide. We wanted to hike out to Timber Island with the puppies. In order to reach the island we first had to cross a river with a precarious rocky bottom and a noticeable current. The water reached to our knees, threatening to topple me. Finley and Bo easily and eagerly swam across. We hiked the perimeter of this rocky island, stopping to admire its magnificent views. Pippa found a couple of sturdy sticks which we used as walking sticks for a steadier return across the river.

On average dogs sleep twelve hours a day, due to their irregular sleep patterns and short REM cycles. Gloriously tired, Finley and Bo slept longer than usual, only really rousing to have their evening meal.

Hugging in sheer delight.

Finley and Bo at play.

Bo is smiling

Canoeing on the Sudbury River.

Canoeing on the Sudbury and Concord Rivers

October 15, 2020

🐾

The Sudbury and Concord Rivers rise in adjoining swamps, and then take wildly disparate paths through Thoreau country until the meet to form the Concord.

—Ann Zwinger and Edwin Way Teal

I wanted to have Finley experience the quiet beauty of two of our local rivers while sitting on the bottom of a canoe, but I didn't know how he would react. Would he get scared and rock the boat to the extent that we would capsize, or might he just leap into the boat and remain quiet throughout our journey? Finley was properly outfitted with a life jacket which he didn't like from the beginning; his first tryout being the week before. I held my breath as I coaxed him into the canoe. He landed between the crossbars and sat quietly. The photo of him decked out in his orange preserver could have landed him on the cover of the L.L. Bean catalog. No prejudice here of course.

It was a perfectly gorgeous Sunday afternoon. We passed quite a few kayakers and canoeists as we paddled downstream. At least 50 percent of them noticed Finley and exclaimed a similar version of: "How did you get your dog to that?"

I replied, "I have no idea. This is his maiden voyage!" We passed under the North Bridge, colloquially known as "the Old North Bridge." It is an approximate replica of the 1760 bridge, present during the Battle of Lexington and Concord. Soon we reversed direction and headed for Egg Rock, a picturesque promontory marking the confluence of the Sudbury, Assabet, and Concord rivers. Attached to Egg Rock is a metal plaque inscribed with the following words:

> ON THE HILL NASHAWTUCK THE MEETING OF THE RIVERS AND ALONG THE BANKS LIVED THE INDIAN OWNERS MUSKETAQUID BEFORE THE WHITE MEN CAME

The word *Musketaquid* is an Algonquin word for "grassy plain" and was used to describe the pastoral nature of the Sudbury and Concord rivers. Native Americans used these rivers for transportation and food.

Our canoe was admirably slow and silent, getting us to places that feet cannot reach. Finley notably fell asleep that afternoon, his big head resting on one of the canoe's crossbars. Our river trail felt like an alluring waterway as we paddled through colorful reflections, magically enhancing the views of Little Blue Herons walking along the muddy shore. We felt refreshed.

Finley loved every minute of his latest adventure. Once we swept our canoe in for a landing at Calf Pasture, I took off his life jacket and he was free once again. A few steps later, Finley was in the Sudbury River for a well-deserved afternoon swim.

The inscription on Egg Rock

Finley and friend at the Old North Bridge

Three Adventures in Ten Hours

October 22, 2020

🐾

Dogs not only make us feel better, they actually make us better. Studies show that contact with canines can help lower cholesterol and blood pressure, decrease the risk of heart disease, strengthen the immune system, and reduce levels of stress, anxiety and depression.

—Martha M. Everett

My brother flew in from Miami last week and asked me outright if he could participate in a Finley adventure. I queried, "How about having three adventures in one day, the first one being in New Hampshire?" He was in!

Finley had never crossed the border into the "Live Free or Die" state (also known as the Granite State). He took no notice when we did.

I plotted a backroads loop around Mt. Monadnock, in southern NH. In a lake reflecting this prominent mountain, Finley did as Finley does; he leaped into the water. He swam around, while my brother and I stood in the sunshine, admiring the view. We saw what looked to be black dots moving up the bare metamorphic rock toward the peak. At an elevation of 3165 feet, Mt. Monadnock stands alone. It is the second most climbed mountain in the world, the first being Mt. Fuji, one of Japan's three holy mountains. Because of its proximity to Boston, (62 miles northwest.) and other population centers, 125,000 hikers summit the mountain every year, so you will never be alone. Go anyway. Having twice climbed the mountain, I can say that the views from the top are breathtaking. On a clear day, you can see all six New England states."

Finley and my brother and I found an open field nearby for an early afternoon picnic. Finley shared in some of my peanut butter and strawberry conserve, orange and lavender sandwich.

We crossed back into Massachusetts to visit the Lazlo Family Farm in Ashby. I met Clark Lazlo at Russell's Farmer's Market in Wayland, where he sold fresh biscuits and other special treats for dogs. He invited Finley and me for a private tour of his twenty-seven-acre livestock farm. He mentioned that Finley could be unleashed while visiting his horses and the pigs. Clark's caveat was that Finley had to be leashed while visiting his flock of Navajo-Churro sheep, because they would be terrified of Finley, their perceived predator. When Finley stood before them, he tugged on his leash, wanting to engage with this woolly new species. Eventually he gave up and just stared at them, without so much as a bark. Before taking our leave of Clark Lazlo's bucolic farm, I learned that he would be participating in Russell's Winter Farmers Market.

Our last adventure of the day found us at Trap Falls in Willard Brook State Forest. Finley ran the short distance to the falls, which at this time of year, flowed at a trickle. I envisioned the picturesque setting before me filled in with a high volume of water, only to be experienced in the spring. We will return then. Low water or high water, Finley is and will continue to be one happy puppy.

Finley observes Navajo-Churro sheep.

Finley swims close to Mt. Monadnock.

Finley Revisits Wright Woods in Autumn

October 29, 2020

Nature provides a lovely backdrop for Finley.

The belief that dogs are color-blind is a common misperception.
Dogs actually do see color, but many fewer colors than humans do.
—Jay Neitz

Our first frost of the season took place in the early hours of October 18. At seven thirty, Finley and I set out for Wright Woods in Concord. On the way, we drove by fog-covered streams and wetlands that created scenes of ethereal beauty. I opened the car's windows for brief periods so that Finley could take in all the wonderful smells. We were planning on meeting a friend who would be bringing cups of honeyed mint tea, while I would supply us with freshly-baked mixed-berry scones from Verrill Farm, always a favorite. Liver treats are considered by many people as the best training treats for dogs, and I was ready with a handful of them for Finley to enjoy, though, this time, without the required quid pro quo. Since we three would be sitting down at the concrete base of the old stone boathouse to enjoy our delectables, I figured that if Finley had the aforementioned stinky treats to keep him busy, he would keep away from my scone!

We arrived at the boathouse and marveled at the bright scenery.

In his 1859 natural history essay entitled "Autumnal Tints," Thoreau wrote the following: "Europeans coming to America are surprised by the brilliancy of our autumnal foliage. There is no account of such a phenomenon in English poetry, because the trees acquire but few bright colors there." When referring to our own foliage, Thoreau went on to write, "October is the month for painted leaves."

I often wondered what colors my dogs would see best, knowing that dogs don't only see the world in black and white. It was time to learn more. Dogs see shades of blues and yellows. The color comparison chart shows, that Finley would be unable to see the red and orange colors of the leaves. He would only see them in yellow.

It is nice to know however, that Finley's-eye view of the world is more colorful than many of us had believed before.

PS. An odd fact is that the most popular dog toys today are red or orange. It makes no sense to me now.

Finley runs out of the Sudbury River.

What a Human Sees

What a Dog Sees

Halloween, 2020 Style

November 5, 2020

🐾

I was working in the lab late one night
When my eyes beheld an eerie sight
For my monster from his slab began to rise
—Bobby "Boris" Pickett, "Monster Mash"

Oh to be frightened on Halloween night! And under a full moon as well! This combination last took place in 1955, but no live being would have been scared of Finley that night, because this gentle dog had transformed into Super Dog!

Halloween, like everything else, looked different this year. The Wayside Inn, while practicing physical distancing, welcomed "all humans and beasts." A drive-by jack-o'-lantern contest was held at Haskell Field. Finley, of course, jumped out of the car and posed for his costumed cameo. Some neighborhoods held block parties that required all pre-bagged candy and dog-treats be placed and spaced on tables near the end of driveways.

Finley was invited by his next-door neighbor and dear friend Lulu (blond golden retriever) to a little gathering on her porch. Lulu's two human-dog-sisters would be there as well. On many days and nights throughout the seasons, Finley would sit on the lawn and stare at Lulu's house, hoping that she would make an appearance, so it would be a special treat for him to see her in her pretty pink tutu.

Finley alighted the broad steps to Lulu's house. In an instant he began to kiss Lulu and her human sisters.

You may wonder about the origins of Halloween. Our festival is derived from the ancient Celtic festival, known as Samhain. It was a time when the veil between the worlds of the living and dead were the thinnest. Beings were able to cross over between the worlds. The Celts had feasts, while honoring their ancestors and showing them hospitality. But not all of the beings were dead ancestors. This was also a night when the faeries could enter the human world, and many of them were mischief-makers. Since people feared certain encounters with the faeries, they wore masks at Samhain to trick the faeries into not recognizing them. They would leave out bowls of milk, or even beer or whisky, in hopes of being left alone by the fairies.

In preparation for our pandemic Halloween, I thought to inquire if Sudbury's very own Chris Evans (Captain America) would be willing to share in a photo with Sudbury's very own Superdog Finley. Perhaps Chris might even be persuaded to share some of his adventures with us. I was sure that many children and grown-ups in town would be elated to see them together in full regalia. Alas, this was not to be. Oh well. Perhaps someday?

Superdog, Tutu-Lulu, and the two human-dogs from Paw Patrol

Finley is kissing Skye, the new dog on the block.

Superdog Finley at the jack-o'-lantern walkthrough at Haskell Field

A Trip to Noon Hill in Medfield

November 12, 2020

🐾

The Charles River has always been at the heart of Massachusetts. It follows the current, beginning at its source in Hopkinton and descending to Boston Harbor. The natural beauty of the river has long been appreciated for its recreational, restorative value. In the early 1800s industrial mills were built at every fall of the river.

—Ron McAdow

It was suggested that Finley and I climb Noon Hill in Medfield at around the tenth of October this year to view its peak foliage. By following the red-dot trail (1:3 miles RT), we would reach the top, a mere 370 feet above the wooded countryside surrounding the Charles River. Finley, my expectant passenger, was about to have a new adventure! We drove south for forty-eight minutes and reached the seven or eight car parking lot when I saw large signs that pronounced: "No overflow parking. Come back again. Forewarned." Luckily for us, there was only one car in the parking lot on that dazzling Monday morning. With an impatient cry, Finley surged out of the car and ran past the kiosk to the start of the trail. He ran back and forth, taking at least ten steps to my one. Then he ran off the trail, past beech and white oak trees that were glowing in the morning light.

The Noon Hill Reservation belongs to the Trustees of the Reservation and is part of the Bay Circuit Trail and Greenway, a 230-mile trail that runs from Newburyport to Duxbury. The trail is an arc of green space that links the parks, rivers, open spaces and historic sight surrounding the outer suburbs of Boston.

When Finley and I reached the summit of Noon Hill, we enjoyed our respective snacks. I poured some cold water from my thermos into Finley's collapsible water bowl. While I surveyed the landscape, Finley went off to investigate this not-so-lofty peak. We were all alone.

Noon Hill is 1.7 miles above the Charles River, but the river was nowhere in sight. Because the hill is so distinct, Medfield's early residents could tell it was dinner time when the sun passed over the hill.

Side trails within the reservation could have extended our hike, though we didn't veer off the red-dot trail that day. Finley and I had a glorious time. When we reached the parking lot, I buckled us up into our seat belts, and we headed due north toward home.

Another history lesson and a fun adventure with Super Dog Finley!

Finley summits Noon Hill in Medfield.

A Little Boy and a Football

November 19, 2020

🐾

Once upon a time there was a girl that really
loved dogs. It was me. The End.
Life happens. Dogs help.
Anything is paw-sible.
—T-shirts seen in the catalog *In the Company of Dogs*

Sometimes Finley and I set out in search of new adventures, and sometimes, during the course of an ordinary walk, new adventures find us. These are some of the most delightful of times because they roll out in such unexpected ways.

Yesterday morning was the start of an Indian summer day, though the temperature was still fifty-two degrees. This kind of warm and much-loved day happens only after the first frost of the season has occurred. Finley and I set out for a walk on the abandoned railbed near our house, when we literally stopped in our tracks, for there on the opposite side of Dudley Brook was a boy who was looking at us. Since we both wore dark red jackets, I thought that the commonality would be a means of striking up a conversation with him. He told me that his name was William and that he was six years old. He said that he liked dogs and wished he could have one.

"If it's okay with you, I could have my dog Finley swim across the brook, but you need to know that Finley will probably want to shake his wet coat all over you."

"Yes" was his reply.

Finley had been quietly standing by my side listening to the conversation when I commanded, "Go say hi." He raced down the hill, jumped into the brook, swam across and ran up the far side of the hill to begin playing with his new friend. After a while, William turned around and looked at me and said, "Are you a grown-up?"

I chuckled to myself and watched the perfect scene of a young boy and a puppy enjoying one another. Finley only returned to me when I called out, "Stick," which is his favorite word.

As he galloped down the railbed, I threw a stick for him to retrieve, but this time the throw was wide. It landed in a huge pile of leaves at the bottom of another short but steep slope. Finley ran down and threw himself into the pile with a fierce determination to find his stick. His tail was the only part of his body that I could see. What a great photograph that would have been, had I taken it!

As if the aforementioned mini adventures weren't enough for the day, Finley managed to sniff out a football in another mound of leaves. Though it is already halfway through the football season, Finley wasted no time in beginning to practice his running game. His ears flapped wildly as he picked up speed. Go, boy! At one point, he closed his eyes, but still he ran.

PS. My friend Anna once wrote, "If our ears flapped and curled like a dogs, we'd be so much more stylish."

Finley jumps out of the creek with a football he found.

A Massage Fit for a Dog

November 26, 2020

🐾

Dogs will delight in even the simplest of activities. I find this one of their most enchanting and endearing qualities. Every walk is thrilling. Every car ride brings the possibility of adventure. Each rub is so pleasurable that it simply must not end.

—Jenny Langbehn

For the past thirty-two years, I have either raised yellow Lab puppies or adopted elderly yellows. All of my Labs have been happy to receive body rubs, tickles, and generalized petting. Being touched has always been a significant pleasure in their lives. Of course, many factors like breed temperament and age will affect a dog's reaction to massage. Some dogs, like humans, react negatively.

I am pleased to report that Finley often smiles during the course of his massages. I smile as well. The shared experience is a natural extension of our love for one another.

On one particular sunny afternoon last week, I spread Finley's favorite blanket out on the grass of my friend's backyard. Since Finley has a passion for being outside, he would have the opportunity to smell the scents of late November while receiving his massage. As you well know, his sense of smell is the sharpest of all his senses, so I expected him to land in "Swoonsville" in about four minutes or less. I too breathed in the scent of freshly fallen leaves, as I prepared my camera to document Finley's massage.

Judy was ready to begin. Finley's full body treatment consisted of a thorough and methodical massage over the entire length of his body. For a simple variation on a regular massage, she put a sock on each hand. The "dog footprint" socks made her hands look cute, though I can't say Finley noticed. With each stroke, this variation was intended to cover more of the surface area of Finley's body.

In a final series of moves, Judy gently lifted the excess skin on the back of Finley's neck and began kneading it. Author Jenny Langbehn suggested that "you sing a rousing rendition of 'That's Amore' as you knead the skin like pizza dough."

Through it all, Finley gracefully accepted his special massage with all of its variations. When it was over, he stood up, wagged his tail and ran off to explore my friend's spacious backyard.

Massage is a wonderful thing.

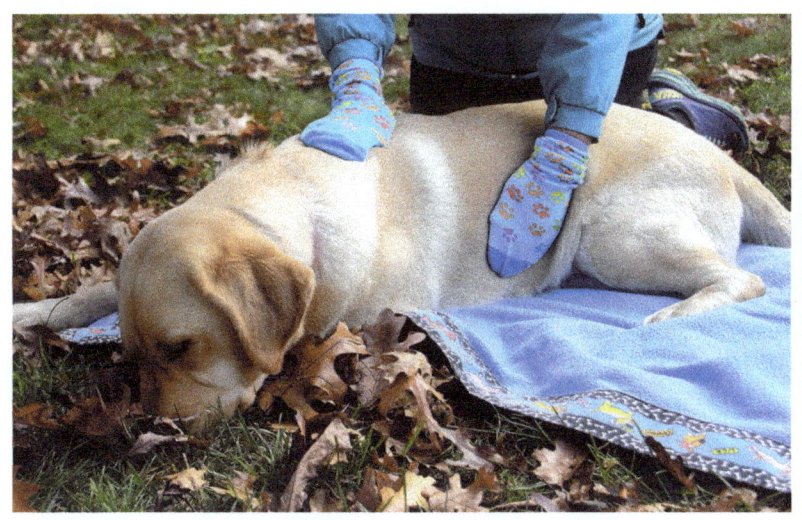

Finley accepts a massage variation.

Finley enjoys his belly rub.

A Visit to Ponyhenge

December 3, 2020

🐾

It's called PONYHENGE—a graveyard of dozens of abandoned rocking horses that stand sentinel on a bucolic pasture in Lincoln. The arrangement often mysteriously changes, and the toy herd's number is constantly growing thanks to community contributions.

—*Boston Magazine*

In cruising down Old Sudbury Road, a back road in the neighboring town of Lincoln, I would typically notice an ever growing number of rocking horses placed in a field off the road. I thought that it might be a good idea for Finley to visit with them if only for me to observe his reaction as he tries to befriend them. When the day arrived, I put Finley's personal red scarf around his thick neck to make him as presentable as possible.

Before the visit and in order to ensure our proper nourishment, we drove to the Whoopie Wagon, stationed at a local garden center. I bought a whoofie pie for Finley and a whoopie pie for me. His pie was made of oatmeal and carrots and was around two and a half inches in diameter. Finley leaned down to sniff his pie and turned away. This was hard to believe because Finley had never refused a food item in his life, with the exception of lettuce.

I queried the server, "Are there refunds for dogs that don't like it?"

He replied, "No, but try breaking it up. That should do it."

I did break up his whoopie pie, but he only reluctantly ate a tiny bit of it. Hopefully the next dog or wild animal that came along would enjoy the rest of Finley's pie! (I must say that I enjoyed my human pie immensely.)

The collection of rocking horses is shrouded in mystery. For the past few years an unknown entity has rearranged the positions of dozens of them, creating a kind of graveyard. Who was that person and how did it happen? Of course, Finley was only interested in meeting these new creatures, so you can well imagine where he first sniffed. It didn't matter if he sniffed a white, pink or blue pony because he came away from them all with no report card. Bored, Finley ran to the edge of the field where he found an outlet that marked the entrance to a narrow woodland path. I hurried after him.

Within a couple of minutes, we came upon a backyard enclosed by a low white picket fence. Standing there were two adults and a child who appeared unsurprised to see us. Perhaps these folks might know the back story of Ponyhenge. In fact, they did, and the story unfolded. Ten years ago the father put his daughter's outgrown rocking horse in a field located within the confines of his two acre property. Soon after that another rocker mysteriously appeared. Much later he learned that his neighbor put out the second rocker. Many more rockers began to appear in all shapes, colors and sizes.

The father went on to say that because he has so many rockers, he has to go to the dump quite often to "thin out the herd." Though it is not advertised, he told me that anyone is welcome to take a rocker!

A couple of weeks later, Finley and I were on the way to Honey Pot Hill Orchards in Stow. We bought a bag of Macoun apples for ourselves and for the horses that he had befriended at Dutton Downs some months ago. We were almost there when suddenly I did a double take, for there on the right side of the road was a collection of six rocking horses in a field, waiting.

All this and heaven too.

Finley poses with the herd.   **Finley and his whoofie pie**

Forest Bathing

December 10, 2020

🐾

We all know that spending time in nature supports us when something is wrong or we are upset. The Forest is the therapist. Linger, linger, linger. Take time to be quiet.
—**Nadine Mazzola,** *Forest Bathing with Your Dog*

Dogs are completely in their senses and guide us to do the same. Isn't that what forest bathing is all about? I read about the plethora of guided walks and zoom talks related to the topic, and so one evening I zoomed in, eager to learn more.

On the way back from the vet's office the other day, Finley and I decided to stop off at the Boy Scout Reservation to do some forest bathing in the waning afternoon light. We took the Pond Trail up to a now-dry vernal pool, and I found a large rock set in the middle of the depression. I sat on the rock and tuned in to Finley and everything else that I could sense in this lovely spot. As a forest detective, Finley went off for his requisite exploration. After about fifteen minutes I invited him to come over and sit by my side and pause. Forest Bathing with Finley makes us even more in tune with each other. We didn't rush. We let ourselves have the complete sensory experience. This is not always easy to do; it can take some effort to remove oneself from all thoughts of civilization.

I remembered the lines of Mary Oliver's famous poem "Wild Geese": "You only have to let the soft animal of your body love what it loves. The sun and the clear pebbles of the rain are moving across the landscape."

I brought myself back to my senses, and I put my arm around Finley's neck. With his head up he smelled the fresh air as I began to align my breath with his.

The forest bathing recipe is as follows: A regular walk with your dog is most often what people do, but if you have the time and inclination, let the magic begin. Walk slowly, find a spot that feels right and stand or sit with your loyal companion, allowing yourself to let the woods enter your being with your senses alive. You might want to go back in time and even become five years old again. Play silly games or build a house of twigs and pine cones for the little creatures. And then watch your dog destroy the little house that you built!

However you choose to forest bathe, be prepared and wear an extra layer of clothing in the cold weather. If you happen to be the parent of a Lab or any other dog that naturally wears two coats, you can save yourself from having to buy an additional one.

Finley enjoys his adventure as a forest bather.

Finley Finds Symbols of Peace

December 17, 2020

🐾

Peace is its own reward.
—Mahatma Ghandhi

Be a pineapple—stand tall, wear a crown
and be sweet on the inside.
—Bryan Anthonys

Peace and pineapples are two important symbols synonymous with the current holiday season, so I decided to take Finley out for a pose and play adventure in front of both a peace barn and a pineapple barn.

The peace barn, located in Lincoln, has a giant peace sign painted on its face. A symbol of the '70s, it recalls the bohemian, magical, and utopian nature of those times. My friend Maddy remembers taking part in dance performances on its "good wooden floors" and reenacting various Greek myths, among them the story of Demeter and Persephone. The barn has been recently renovated and is available to rent as a one-bedroom apartment.

Seated in front of the peace symbol, Finley looks like a small creature, though he is in fact a creature large in stature. If you happen to know the pact that we have, you will recall that whenever Finley poses for me, he will be rewarded with a romp afterward. Back in the car, I informed him that we were on our way to visit another peace barn, but when we arrived, I was surprised to see a pineapple barn instead. This once again illustrates that often our remembrances are not aligned with the facts.

Finley sat before the pineapple barn posing until I released him. He is used to posing, having done so multiple times in his short twenty-three-month existence.

The pineapple is a universal symbol of hospitality. It first appeared in Europe after its discovery in Guadeloupe by Christopher Columbus in 1493. During colonial times it became a coveted commodity that only the wealthy could afford. So sought after was the pineapple that sometimes it was rented to households to serve as the visual apex of their dining room table, thus showing off their supposed rank in society. Only later was this fruit sold to more affluent clients who actually ate it!

Being in a pineapple state of mind, I found that what was left for Finley and me to do was to buy a pineapple and eat it together in peace. It is a good thing to share a tropical fruit on a cold, almost winter's day.

Finley poses in front a peace sign painted on a barn in Lincoln.

Finley sits in front of a barn with a pineapple painted on it.

A snow day is lots of fun for Finley.

Finley loves the snow.

Snow Day!

December 24, 2020

I wonder if the snow loves the trees and fields, that is, kisses them so gently? And then it covers them up snug, you know, with a white quilt; and perhaps it says, "Go to sleep darlings, till the summer comes again."

—Lewis Carroll

The forecast was for powdery snow and lots of it. Finley and I woke up that morning to six inches of fresh snow blanketing the countryside. By 2:00 p.m., a foot had fallen, but I am getting ahead of myself.

Finley stared out one of the sunroom windows, which was low enough to give him a clear view of the great outdoors. He is one of those dogs that loves to look out as the world goes by; in this case I think that all he could see were the snowplows, but I can't be sure of that. This was the kind of snow that delights bigger dogs, children and many adults. Finley's dear friend Gizmo, who is a small dog, a Pug, felt the opposite way. "He refused to go out," his parent plaintively said.

I kicked up some fresh powder in Finley's direction and the fun began. He started to run, looking like a thoroughbred prancing through the snow. Soon he stopped running and lowered his block-shaped head into the snow. He came up with a huge branch, his mouth closed firmly around it. With his front legs extending forward, he began making happy circles in the ever-increasing snow, proud as any creature could be. That he can sniff out a snow-laden branch, retrieve and run with it, continues to be a source of amazement for me. Not to mention that this particular branch weighed at least fifteen pounds!

Soon Finley dropped his branch and looked at me expectantly. I knew that he was ready for a game of fetch. I attempted to oblige, but when I picked up the heavy branch and tried to throw it, I slipped backward and landed on my posterior, while my glove flew off my left hand and traced a really beautiful upward arc. For some reason Finley didn't see this, for if he had? You know the rest.

Like a typical three-year-old human child, Finley didn't want to come indoors just yet. Forget about it! When we finally did, I knew that we needed to ingest extra calories to compensate for our cold-weather exertions. I ate a large piece of chocolate cake while Finley enjoyed two canine beef jerkies.

I think that we should reward ourselves for what we do.

Finley Discovers Ford's Folly in Framingham

December 31, 2020

🐾

Of all the follies that the elder generation
falls victim to, this is the most foolish.
—Henry Ford

What in the world is Ford's Folly? Having lived in Sudbury for over forty years, I could not answer the question even though the site, located deep in the woods, was less than four miles from my house.

On one late November morning Finley and I set out to explore the Wittenborg Woods in Framingham. Having taken a picture of the map, I unhappily noted that the trails had no markers at any of the intersections.

After trying to memorize the paths that we had taken, we encountered a youngish woman who said that we were near Ford's Folly, although she couldn't say what it was. Finley and I headed off to find it.

I gasped when I saw Ford's Folly, and Finley turned to look at me, a little concerned.

Set out before us was a stone dam that was thirty feet high and ninety feet long. It was built by Henry Ford in 1923 in the traditional manner, using local stone, manpower and oxen.

The dam was planned to create a reservoir from a small stream that runs down the hill from nearby Nobscot Mountain.

The reservoir was intended to store extra water to run the Grist Mill in the Wayside Inn complex.

The problem was that the reservoir could not hold water because the bedrock was porous.

What a folly; a dam that holds no water and serves no purpose! Finley and I safely walked across the top of the dam eventually making our way back to our car.

After the foot of snow that Sudbury received, Finley and I returned to the folly, this time armed with the knowledge of its interesting history.

Finley hopped through the snow while I snowshoed behind. Deer tracks were etched into the snowy landscape.

We passed the stream that was meant to feed the reservoir and Finley dropped down into it to cool off. We reached the dam and he began to explore the area beneath it.

A week later I asked Finley if he wanted to go back to Ford's Folly for the third time, this time with the addition of Tucker, Finley's newest friend, a five-month-old Norwegian Elkhound.

Finley, with his tail whipping from side to side, showed me that he would be delighted to return. Being as openhearted as he is, Finley has many friends.

In any case, Tucker's mom, Andrea, told me that when she was a young child her family owned a black-and-silver-coated German shepherd when the most common German shepherd of the 1950s had a black-and-gold-colored coat.

The shepherds were a protective and very popular breed in those days. She went on to say that *her* shepherd was a littermate of the famous Rin Tin Tin who had his own television show, which ran from 1954 to 1959. The Rin Tin Tin stories were about the mutual devotion between a boy and his dog and the many adventures that they shared.

Finley and Tucker had a blast frolicking in the snow, with the stone dam serving as their beautifully constructed backdrop.

I thought of the workmen building this structure ninety-eight years ago, and hoped that they weren't too upset when they learned that their hard work was all in vain.

Finley and Tucker are playing beneath the dam.

Finley is in the stream that feeds Ford's Folly.

A Trip to Vermont

January 7, 2021

🐾

Icy finger waves, ski trails on a
mountainside, snowlight in Vermont
—John Blackburn, "Moonlight in Vermont"

I have always felt a strong connection to the beautiful landscape of Vermont, with its mountains, rolling hills, clear lakes, hospitable people and social and environmental values. Did I mention the scenic views at practically every turn?

It was therefore necessary that Finley see all this for himself. He already had two adventures in northern New England, one in New Hampshire and one in Maine, which he enjoyed immensely. My friends and I had been properly quarantined and COVID tested. Finley and I were ready to go. When we crossed the New Hampshire border into Vermont, I began to hum "Moonlight in Vermont" and immediately heard Finley's otter tail vigorously slapping the backseat. I told him that he too was an incurable romantic.

Finley and I had planned a five-day trip to northwestern Vermont where we would be staying in a dog-friendly inn with each of the four suites having its own separate entrance. We were due to meet our Connecticut friends and Bo, their now seven-month-old yellow Labrador, Finley's unofficial cousin and dear friend.

"It is a different set of four walls," pronounced my friend David upon our arrival.

Finley and Bo ran to greet each other, and they played mostly nonstop for five days till exhaustion set in. After familiarizing himself with our premises, Finley settled into a leather settee, the best seat of all. It was perfectly situated under a large picture window which framed Lake Champlain, a gigantic lake formed from melting glacial waters, and the Adirondack Mountains of New York, farther to the west. Our inn stood on a hillside, shadowed by the Green Mountains of Vermont. It is interesting to note the differences between the two mountain ranges. Essentially, the Adirondacks are about a mile high, much taller than the Green Mountains, and they form a circular dome 160 miles in diameter. The Green Mountains are an elongated range forming the spine of Vermont and running from north to south for 250 miles.

Directly behind the inn was Mt. Philo State Park, the smallest of Vermont's state parks. Finley and Bo ran ahead of us on the snowy trail as we set out to climb Mt. Philo, a peak reaching 968 feet into the sky. If we subtract 354 feet, which was our starting elevation, we climbed a grand total of 614 feet! With his muscular fortitude, Finley could have effortlessly climbed Mt. Washington in New Hampshire, a mountain over ten times higher than Mt. Philo.

By 4:00 p.m. we humans were standing around a huge bonfire, warming ourselves after our easy climb. Finley and Bo continuously and delightedly tackled each other. More often than not Bo threw Finley to the ground, scrambling to keep him there. Bo weighs fifty-five pounds and Finley weighs ninety-three pounds.

That night, Bo jumped up onto the settee to be near his friend. The sky was now clear. I do believe that the boys were as thrilled as I was to see the moon setting into the Adirondacks beyond the lake.

Finley enjoys the bonfire while in Vermont.

Finley rests on the settee overlooking the Adirondacks.

Finley summits his first mountain.

A Visit to Great Brook Farm

January 14, 2021

🐾

My fashion philosophy is, if you're not covered in dog hair, your life is empty.
—Elayne Boosler

Although it was a very cold morning, I opened the car windows as we approached Great Brook Farm State Park in Carlisle. Finley strained at his seat belt, his nose twitching as he inhaled the earthy smells of the barnyard. He whimpered in excitement as he alighted from our car.

Agriculture has been a major part of this attractive landscape for centuries. Native American sacred sites have been found here, and seventeenth-century cellar holes were discovered from early colonial settlements. In 1967, the thousand-acre state park was formed.

Before setting out on a trail, my friend Sophie and Finley and I visited with the barnyard animals. Finley sat quietly as he looked toward all these newfangled animals: an assortment of cows, llamas, chickens and goats. I noticed that a young llama and Finley exchanged gazes for quite a few seconds. As you may recall, Finley had already met and in some cases befriended a string of horses, a flock of sheep and a potbelly pig.

We were lucky in our choice to walk the one-mile Lantern Loop trail, which beckoned us through rolling fields. There are twenty miles of wooded and open trails to choose from in this gem of a park. The Lantern Loop trail is so named because lanterns line the pathways for night time cross-country skiing. Imagine coming here to "kick and glide" under a full moon? The downside to skiing on machine made ski tracks is that your canine companion is not permitted to join you.

After completing the loop, we naturally found ourselves standing in front of the ice cream shop across from the barn. It was closed for the season but it shouldn't have been, for we hearty New Englanders do enjoy our ice cream in all seasons!

When Finley and I return in the spring, I will be sure to bring some Yopup for him:
"a delectable frozen yogurt cup, made with apple juice and cheddar cheese."
He will not give himself time to savor it; Finley undoubtedly will swallow it whole.

Finley runs by the pond at Great Brook Farm in Carlisle.

The Pup Turns Two

January 21, 2021

🐾

My dog practices 15 minutes of transcendental meditation daily and can transport himself to a blissful state of serenity at a moment's notice. He is also a Reiki healer and a licensed acupuncturist, graciously in-network with all major pet-insurance providers. My dog cannot speak, of course. But he has told me through telepathy that he'd be happy to give your dog a free consultation.

—Danielle Kraese

The festivities were about to begin. Finley and I began the day with a party in celebration of his second birthday. I placed the "king for a day" crown on his furry head. As he posed for the obligatory photo, he fell asleep waiting for me to signal my okay for him to eat his special pup cake. Made of a mixture of eighty-five percent cooked hamburger meat and steel cut oats, the cake was quickly devoured.

Puppies mature into adults at different times. A large dog breed will mature into an adult at about fifteen months, while smaller breeds will remain puppies for only about nine months. Many experts do not consider a Lab puppy to be fully grown up till they are two and a half years old. I suspect that Finley will remain puppyish for years to come.

After digesting his cake, Finley and I headed out to Hop Brook to hang out at one of his favorite cascading waterfalls. The recent rain provided us with a stronger current then is typical for mid-January. From an embankment several feet downstream from the falls, I threw a nice fat stick, positioning it to land at the bottom of the falls. Finley hurled himself into the water and swam hard but was not able to advance. With encouragement, Finley powered through the current, retrieved the stick and turned around to look at me. I called out my approval for his brave, strong swim. He beamed.

When Finley swam back toward me, he had a little trouble climbing up the embankment. I called out, "C'mon, Finley; *you* can do it!"

And so he did. He looked at me once again, making sure that I saw his latest achievement. Lenny Bruce, a stand-up comedian and social critic, once said, "The whole motivation for any performer: Look at me ma."

Before dinner that night, Finley and I played a game of Blueberry Catch. He caught twenty-four blueberries in a row. Perhaps he will beat this score the next time we play.

Finley wears his birthday crown.

Finley hurls himself into the stream.

A New Equine Friend

January 28, 2021

🐾

I was therefore unprepared for the expression in Blue's [eyes]. Blue was lonely. Blue was horribly lonely and bored. I was not shocked that this should be the case; five acres to tramp by yourself, endlessly, even in the most beautiful of meadows—and his was—cannot provide many interesting events. … No, I was shocked that I had forgotten that human animals as well as nonhuman animals can communicate quite well; if we are brought up around animals as children we take this for granted.

—Alice Walker, "Am I Blue?"

A horse came into our lives quite by accident. I had heard about Prairie, who unfortunately could relate to Blue's sad story because she too is a lonely horse.

Her two dearest friends recently disappeared from her life: Jakie, through death, and Target, through a move to another horse farm.

Might not Finley and I help to alleviate some of Prairie's sorrow by visiting with her?

We were given permission to enter her paddock.

Since Prairie was used to having dogs around, I was told that having Finley close by would not pose a problem.

Prairie, a semiwild Nokota horse, is predominately black.

Her parents, living wild and free, hail from the Badlands of the northern plains, specifically from a region in North Dakota.

The unique Nokota horses are known as the horses of the nomadic Sioux Indian tribe who would keep them in their tepees after dark, so as not to have them stolen by neighboring tribes.

Bearing gifts of sliced apples and carrots, Finley and I approached Prairie's paddock.

Having undoubtedly smelled the goodies, Prairie was waiting for us at the gate. I was immediately struck by her beautiful face. I called out to her, "You are a black beauty!"

Finley slipped under her gate, found Prairie's horse ball and began running around and pushing the ball forward with his nose, while Prairie watched him intently, probably wondering about the origin of this strange and new character.

Finley visits with Prairie once a week now, while I continue with two more weekly visits. Of course, we three are always happy to see one another again.

Additional news has come our way. In the spring, Prairie is due to have a companion join her in her paddock!

PS. The classic autobiography *Black Beauty* was written by Anna Sewell in 1877. The book stressed the importance of kindness toward animals. The story was adapted into a number of films over the years; the 1994 version was true to the original story, while the 2020 version not only changed the story but also turned Black Beauty, who was a female horse, into a male horse.

Finley and Prairie greet one another

A Romp in the Snow

February 4, 2021

🐾

Slow down, you move too fast
You got to make the morning last
Just kicking down the cobblestones
Looking for fun and feeling groovy
— "The Fifty-Ninth Street St. Bridge Song
(Feelin' Groovy)," lyrics by Paul Simon

A thick layer of powdery snow had fallen during the night. Finley and I awoke at seven in the face of what would likely be a beautiful day. The arctic blast wasn't due to arrive for another forty-eight hours.

Instead of revisiting our usual haunts, Finley and I were going to travel elsewhere today. As we backed out of our gravel driveway, I told him that we were going to explore Davis Field and find lots of dogs running and playing in the snow. I had visited Davis Field many Labs ago, and like so many other large and open-spaced conservation areas, Davis Field is a place where dogs congregate and frolic together in bliss.

The field is sprawling; the main path follows its perimeter and is located underneath mature evergreen trees now laden with snow. Beyond the evergreens are privately owned hayfields.

Finley surveyed the scene, observing dogs running on and mostly off the path. Not needing a cue from me, he sped off to join them, chasing them at first and then enticing his new acquaintances to follow suit. The sun's rays glinted off the multifaceted snow crystals. When Finley returned to check up on me, I found myself kicking up some powder into his face. He adored this new game and so I continued playing it with him.

In time he ran off to continue making merry with a new crop of smiling dogs, while I began to engage in flights of fancy, a magical mystery tour with Finley being the center of attention, of course. Instead of kicking up the snow in Davis Field, Finley was standing underneath the Fifty-Ninth Street Bridge ("feelin' groovy") in Manhattan, "just kicking down the cobblestones," right next to Paul Simon who was writing his classic song.

"No, that wouldn't do, Finley; you are a country dog! Perhaps a swim off the ledges in Northern Ireland would be more to your liking? My goodness, Finley, where might we go for our next adventure? Well, how about some wheelies in the parking lot?"

"For joy," he answered.

PS. "Davis Field is a great place to sit outside with an adult drink… considering all the bars are closed" (copied from an online review).

Finley catches some snow.

A Return Visit to Wright Woods

February 11, 2021

I like adventures, and I'm going to find some.
—Louisa May Alcott

My friend, Finley, and I planned on walking the big loop at Wright Woods in Concord. With a couple of inches of packed snow on the ground, it would be a pleasant ninety-minute stroll.

After following Finley for a short distance, I saw him veering off the main path to a secondary trail that led down to the nineteenth century stone boathouse on Fairhaven Bay. As a born water dog, Finley smelled the water in the bay, or in this case, the solid ice.

Since we had visited the handsome boathouse in the glorious month of October, we were inclined to follow him. Fairhaven Bay, the widest part of the Sudbury River, is a tranquil seventy-acre bay where Thoreau rowed, sailed and ice skated, having walked to the bay from his house on Walden Pond.

We reached the boathouse. Finley spotted a group of ice fishermen about fifty yards out across the ice and headed out to say hi. I grabbed his favorite object and emphatically called out, "Stick!" He then turned around and ran back to shore. The ice fishermen were having a party, loud rock music circling out from their tent. One of the men was measuring the depth of the ice with an auger. What was the depth of the ice and what was the minimum number of inches required to keep them safe? The ice measured seven inches deep. Way out in the bay, three silhouetted figures were walking across the ice, but Finley didn't notice.

Meanwhile, on the other side of the boathouse and partway up a hill, my friend, who was standing behind a perfectly formed stone wall, called out for us to join her. We found a stairway through an opening in the trees. We climbed the staircase and reached a large patio that provided us with an excellent view of the bay below. My friend and Finley cavorted on the patio when suddenly she slipped and fell forward. True to his nature, Finley raced to her; stick in mouth, for the rescue. Had he been able to transform himself into a St. Bernard, he would have worn a small barrel of brandy around his neck to deliver this warming drink to avalanche victims, etc. My friend would have laughed even harder had a St. Bernard appeared on the scene.

The truth is that drinking brandy in very cold weather is medically unsound advice because the warming effect is an illusion. Alcohol brings blood closer to the skin and can actually lower body temperature. The story of the St. Bernard and the brandy barrel is pure myth. The monks of St. Bernard trained some of their dogs to carry milk, never brandy, in their rescue operations in the Swiss Alps.

We didn't continue with the rest of our walk that morning; instead, we concluded our adventure on the patio overlooking Fairhaven Bay.

PS. Online charts indicate that four inches of ice is suitable for ice fishing and walking, but ice thickness varies from spot to spot, so do be careful.

Finley is on the ice by some ice fishermen.

Finley revels in his first Nor'easter.

First Nor'easter Brightened This Dog's Day

February 18, 2021

🐾

The storm matched the general profile of a Nor'easter, since it moved along the east coast with powerful winds blowing in from the northeast.
—*Wall Street Journal*, **February 4, 2021**

It snowed all night long; large flakes were highlighted by the small pink lights strung around the backyard bird feeders and halfway up the Kousa Dogwood. Three different yardstick readings showed that the snow was seventeen inches deep. I knew that Finley would be thrilled.

It was early in the morning when Finley stood in the driveway surveying the quiet landscape. Soon he ran to the edge of the driveway, leaped over the snow wall created by the snowplow, and found himself in snow that reached up to his shoulders. Fixed to the spot, he whimpered, not knowing what to do next.

I encouraged him to move forward: "Let's go!"

He turned his big head toward me.

I was surprised to see such a worried look in his eyes. "It looks like I will have to rescue you, my boy," I said. Only when I took a couple of steps in his direction did he regain his composure; he started to barrel through the snow, powder flying everywhere. The scene was special, worthy of being viewed by all the Instagramers out there who would delight in watching videos of animals playing in deep snow.

After breakfast, I strapped on my snowshoes, readying to go out with Finley for a jaunt to the backyard, through the woods and on up to the abandoned rail bed. At that intersection, I planned on reversing direction and heading back for more Finley play in the broad expanse of our yard. This plan never came to fruition. I had to agree with Robert Burns that "the best laid schemes o' mice an' men."

Instead of the snowshoes sinking just a few inches into the snow, as they ordinarily do, they sank much deeper than that, causing me to fall. Finley suddenly appeared and jumped on me, the full force of his body driving me deeper into the snow. He thought that this was a new game for us to play. With great difficulty, I managed to get up and take off my snowshoes. My new goal now was to walk to the bird feeders and brush off the accumulated snow, which would allow the birds to continue to feed on the suet and seed that make it easier for them to survive the winter. Using ski poles for balance, I trudged through the snow to reach the feeders. In the meantime, Finley continued to leap and hop through the snow, providing no barrier to his unmitigated strength.

Oh, Finley, if we could trade places for *just* this morning; I would love to drink in the full measure of your new and spectacular experience!

Finley jumps over a bench after the snowfall.

A Visit to White Pond

February 25, 2021

🐾

We went to White Pond, a pretty little Indian bath, lonely now as Walden was, we could almost see the sachem in his canoe in a shadowy cove … Making the circuit of the lake on the shore, we saw marvelous reflections of the colored woods in the water of such singular beauty and novelty that they held us fast to the spot almost to the going down of the sun.
—Ralph Waldo Emerson writes about a walk with
Ellery Channing on October 28, 1848

The name Sachem's Cove (Chief's Cove) in Concord was given to the most remote section of White Pond. Finley and Reggie, one of Finley's dear friends, were going to trek out to the cove amid the crisp new snow. Karla, Reggie's parent, well versed in the trail system that crisscrossed these woods, was going to lead us there. I was looking forward to this hike since I had often heard about the beauty of the pond but never managed to visit.

Two-and-a-half-year-old Reggie is an adorable combination of West Highland Terrier, Maltese, Labrador and shih-tzu. The boys met in the local woods when Finley was an eight-week-old butterball and Reggie was four months old. Animals can fall in love at first sight just like us. Such was the case with Finley and Reggie. Karla told me that whenever Reggie sees/smells our car, he races down the path to find Finley, though we might be a quarter of a mile away.

We humans needed our snowshoes and poles, but unthinkingly didn't bring them. After a ten-minute slog through the deep snow, with Finley being the only cheerful one among us, we turned back. I was determined to get to the pond, so we drove to a tiny parking area about three miles to the east; it opened to a short trail just above the cove. The sight of the glistening snow, the royal blue sky, the view of the quietly alluring cove, the picture of Finley and Reggie excitedly leaping through the snow (Reggie's short legs made it a little difficult for him) and the distant sound of woodpeckers were all thrilling.

Ralph Waldo Emerson's good friend Henry David Thoreau lived in a cabin that he built on the shores of nearby Walden Pond. Though that pond was made famous by his writings, he was very familiar with White Pond. He reached the same conclusion as Emerson when he wrote: "Since the woodcutter, the railroad, and I myself have profaned Walden, perhaps the most attractive, the gem of the woods is White Pond."

Another discovery, another adventure for "mighty Finley." As you might know, he *adores* the winter, but many folks don't have a double coat like he does, and so they yearn for the arrival of spring ... when it comes.

Finley and Reggie are ready to go.

Finley sniffs the air in Sachem's Cove.

Finley is playing in Danforth Falls in Hudson.

A Return Visit to Danforth Falls

March 4, 2021

🐾

One visit to each waterfall is not enough. If you have visited a particular waterfall only once, you have not really grasped its personality. To see its true character, you must visit in different seasons and during different conditions. Check out the falls during dry and wet weather, when they're covered in snow or during fall foliage.

—Greg Parsons and Kate B. Watson, *New England Waterfalls*

One of the reasons that Finley is fond of waterfalls is because he relishes cold water. The fresh scent of fast-moving water and the gurgling or crashing sound of a New England cascade give him pleasure.

Danforth Falls drops a mere six feet in its entirety and is reachable via a short path from the parking area. There is no formula to record beauty, based on the height of a waterfall, so I wasn't at all surprised to find such a visually charming waterfall. Finley saw a stick lying on a boulder at the bottom of the falls, and he naturally jumped in to retrieve it.

While being entertained by Finley's activities in the falls, my mind began to drift off. The medium of water now under my lens.

The chemically charged negative ions created by moving water and other sources make us feel better overall. The early Europeans spoke of the element of water as a connection to our emotions, often giving us the courage to face our deepest feelings. The pagan author Starhawk asks us to find "the calm pools of tranquility within you ... to sink deep into the well ... below consciousness." Captivated by our newly found treasure, Finley and I lingered at the falls. It was all ours for the length of time we remained.

We decided to return to Danforth Falls after a few more inches of snow fell, which would give the falls a different look. Because of our very snowy February, we didn't have to wait long. When we returned a second time, Finley and I saw the pillowy snow covering the falls, and together we drank in all the life-giving benefits provided by Mother Nature.

PS. We in New England are lucky to have at least five hundred waterfalls to visit. To reduce the likelihood of visiting a dried up waterfall, go before the middle of June.

A Giant Snow Woman

March 11, 2021
🐾

According to Guinness World Records, residents of Bethel, Maine, and surrounding towns built a snow woman measuring 37.21 meters (122.1 feet) tall over a period of one month, completing her on February 26, 2008. Thirteen million pounds of snow were used to build Olympia the snow woman.

On February 24, the outdoor temperature reached fifty degrees, and the next day was much the same. Our typical January thaw took place in late February. As a result of those lovely warm days, the top inch of snow melted and quickly refroze once the temperature slid to below freezing again. Our woodland paths became sheets of rutted ice. One morning in early March, as if to add insult to injury, the wind chill reading was five degrees below zero.

Finley and I were walking that morning as usual. He wore no clothes, and I was outfitted with long underwear, mittens with glove liners, smart wool socks, winter hiking boots, a wool hat with flaps and a grey jacket filled with so much down that I looked like the Michelin Man. Finley and I spotted the tall snow woman at the same time. She was standing right in the middle of Duck Pond. Finley was furious. How dare this being intrude on what he came to believe was *his* pond! After all, he had circumnavigated Duck Pond numerous times. Knowing that the ice was thick enough for us to safely walk out to the snow woman, I commanded Finley: "go say hi!" Finley surveyed the long sticks that served as the snow woman's arms, desperately wanting them. He stretched out his long torso, but fell just short of his goal. I tried to tempt him away with liver treats, his favorite snack, but he would have none of it.

I enjoined him: "Finley, you can't munch on the arms of this beautiful snow woman; it's someone else's creation!" I leashed him and we trotted over to the other side of the pond, during which time he repeatedly looked back and cried. "I'm sorry dear pup," I said.

A small block of ice had dislodged near shore which gave me an idea. Encouraging him to fetch the ice block might distract him and feed his persistent need to retrieve. It worked; his tail began to wag and he was happy once again.

How could Finley run on ice, while I was so dependent on my Yaktrax (traction cleats for ice and snow) or my heavy duty micro spikes that were better for climbing ice covered hills? Having a thick layer of fatty tissue, Finley's foot pads provide him with the ability to maneuver in slippery conditions and also allow him to tolerate temperature extremes.

When it is very dry and cold, his pads sometimes develop hairline cracks; I then apply a waxy substance called Musher's Secret to soften and protect them. Finley always naps after a hardy morning's walk or swim. On this particular day, I gave him a paw massage, which is supposed to relax many dogs. Finley gently snored right through it.

Finley attempts to retrieve the snow woman's arms.

Finley and Dudley are rough-housing.

Visiting Hazel Brook Conservation Land

March 18, 2021

🐾

Hazel Brook and its surrounding areas are a prime example of the domino effect in land protection. Gifts from one or two landowners encouraged others to also protect land along the brook's course, starting with its headwaters and continuing in a patchwork of SVT parcels and conservation restrictions as the brook flows toward the Sudbury River.
—Sudbury Valley Trustees property description

Hazel Brook Conservation Area is on the recommended list of the Sudbury Valley Trustees properties, so in keeping with our need to explore new areas, Finley and I felt that it was time to hike Hazel Brook. On Wednesday mornings Finley has a standing date with his buddy Tucker, a seven-month-old Norwegian Elkhound puppy. When I mentioned his buddy's name, Finley stood up in the backseat of our car, ready to rock and roll.

We parked on the side of the road near the entrance to the woods. A picturesque pond at the beginning of the trail drew Finley in, while Tucker, a non-swimmer, stood on shore wagging his tail and paying close attention to Finley. After a few minutes, Tucker began barking, wanting Finley to resume their play. Soon we began to hear the sound of Hazel Brook bubbling out from the pond. By no means even close in size to one of the ten tributaries of the Sudbury River, it contributes nevertheless to the strength of the river.

Finley and Tucker scampered down the rolling path ahead and soon encountered Dudley, the puppy who became their newest acquaintance. The three puppies began a session of uproarious play.

Leslie, Dudley's parent, eventually joined us; we humans fell into an easy camaraderie that often takes place in the woods when our respective pups are having a blast.

Leslie asked if we had come across the Christmas tree. She explained that people come from all over and at all times, especially in December, to decorate the tree. "Nobody knows how it got started and there is no one in charge," she continued. Intrigued, I asked if she would take us there on our next visit to Hazel Brook.

On our next visit we walked straight out to the tree, located deep into the woods. Finley stared at it, looking up at the branches that were holding all manner of colorful decorations. What a feast for his tender brown eyes. He reached for a shiny red bauble, and before I could say, "F–I–N—," he had it in his mouth and began to chomp. I heard a distinct cracking sound. "Oh, Finley, you're incorrigible!"

I just finished placing an order for a dozen red, round, shiny, and *shatterproof* Christmas tree trinkets; maybe I'll even bring a step ladder to secure them on the tree's middle branches, way above Finley's reach.

Finley is standing under the Christmas tree

A Visit to the Haynes Garrison House

March 25, 2021

🐾

King Philip's War, one of the most significant wars ever fought in North America, lasted in southern New England from June 1675 to August 1676. In this war an alliance of hostile Native American tribes attempted to eliminate all of the English Colonies in New England by killing or driving out all of the immigrant Colonial residents so that the Native Americans could regain control of their former lands.
—notes from King Philip's War and the Sudbury Fight

Finley is a curious creature. I first told him about the importance of the war during one of his early adventures (6/18/20) in the King Philip Woods of Sudbury. King Philip was the name given by the settlers to the Native American Wampanoag chief, Sachem Metacomet.

Winter was coming to an end, and the morning's warmth made it seem like a good day to tell him the story of the Sudbury Fight. Finley loves to listen to stories and I love to tell them.

"Let's get some exercise first," I said, as we entered the King Philip Woods, a rugged area that includes a pond, a bog, undulating paths and stonewalls and a large formation of rocks standing 100 feet or so above the pond, where one may sit and enjoy a morning coffee. We reached the pond; the ice was melting and Finley was swimming around in the water bordering it.

A side path led us to the remnants of the Haynes Garrison House. Finley posed by its memorial marker and then settled down by my side to hear the rest of the story.

"Finley, it seems that this war is lost in the fog of history; so few people even know about it. Did you know that the Sudbury Fight was a major military engagement, part of which took place right here in our town toward the end of the King Philip War?"

I continued, "Most of the town's residents were able to escape to one of the six garrison or fortified houses, while their homes were burned to the ground by some of the Native American tribes. These tribal members felt that they had to rid the land of the ever-increasing settlers who treated the Native Americans miserably.

"King Philip's warriors attacked this garrison house over a period of thirty-six hours, trying to burn it down. They rolled a cart of burning flax down the hill toward the house, but the cart overturned and never reached the garrison. Imagine that all of this took place 100 years before the battles of Lexington and Concord, the start of the American Revolutionary War! The alliance of hostile tribes was well on its way to reaching its military goals until the time of the Sudbury Fight, which caused a major turning point in the war."

I was about to give Finley the reasons for the Native Americans' tactical failure when I noticed that his eyes were beginning to close.

"Okay, Finley, we'll skip over that part for now. Suffice it to say that *after* the Sudbury Fight, the colonists started to win most of the battles and won the war in southern New England four months later. If the alliance of tribes had won the war, then it is unlikely that our country would resemble the United States as it exists today."

Finley's legs were darting, to and fro as he slept. No doubt he was chasing a group of warriors out of town!

Finley is swimming in the pond at the King Philip Woods.

Finley is standing by the Haynes Garrison House monument.

A Springtime Visit to Wright Woods

April 1, 2021

🐾

Born in Concord, MA in 1817, David Henry Thoreau switched his first and middle names after graduating from Harvard. His legal name, though, was always David Henry. Although most people today pronounce Thoreau's surname with the emphasis on the second syllable, he most likely pronounced it "THOR-oh." Ralph Waldo Emerson's son, Edward, wrote that the accent was on the first syllable, and other friends called him "Mr. Thorough."

—from Mentalfloss.com

Yesterday, Finley and I repeated our jaunt out to the stone boat house on Fairhaven Bay in Concord, he to swim and I to sit and occasionally throw a ball out into the bay to keep him busy and satisfied. I laughed as he leaped from the platform into the water, all his legs flying through the air, only to belly flop into the bay.

The bay was partially covered in light fog, caused by the morning's cold air passing over the warmer water of the bay. We had visited this special place before in mid-October, when the leaves were saturated with the brilliant tints of a New England autumn. We returned in winter, when the ice freeze on the bay was thick enough to carry three ice fishermen, their tent and gear. We watched them drill a hole in the ice, drop a line and fish for bass and perch. The wheel of the year has turned once again, and now we find ourselves in springtime.

"Nature does not hurry yet everything is accomplished," said the Chinese philosopher Lao Tzu.

As you know, Finley's sense of smell is his strongest sense; his large nose twitched as he filled it with the scents coming off the bay and beyond.

I have developed a deep emotional connection to this area, not only for its pristine beauty, but also for its historical connections. Henry David Thoreau, who often frequented the bay, was one of the leading Transcendentalists of his time. Transcendentalism was a mid-19th century New England philosophical movement that believed in the inherent goodness of nature. As I sat there, I believed that I saw Thoreau paddling his canoe in the distance, out beyond where Finley was swimming.

Finley blasted back to the platform to where I sat and shook his wet body all over mine. Really, Finley? It was an inappropriate habit of his.

Both of us were reluctant to leave; initially, we followed the shoreline back. We soon spotted a lone fisherman standing in his boat, his line cast. He was far enough out to discourage Finley from swimming out to greet him, but had I been in that boat instead, I don't doubt that Finley would have swum over and followed me clear across the bay if that is where I wanted to go!

After the summer solstice occurs, Finley and I will return to our spot, he to swim and smell the scents of summer, and I to sit and take it all in.

Finley swims in Fairhaven Bay

Finley jumps in to retrieve his rainbow colored ball

Traveling to Gloucester on Cape Ann

April 8, 2021

🐾

White light flashing every 5 seconds... Eastern Point Lighthouse was erected in 1832 on Gloucester's eastern point to mark the harbor entrance. In addition to the light, there is a lighthouse station, which continues to serve as housing for the U.S. Coastguard. One of the station's more famous occupants was Winslow Homer. The noted artist spent a year living at the light in 1880.

—from Cape Ann information

I knew that Finley and I could not delay our trip to Cape Ann, Good Harbor Beach in particular, for this beach was off limits to resident dogs and visitors from April 1 to October 1, and today was March 29. We decided to leave the forested landscape of home and take the hour's journey north. I packed Finley's dinner, my lunch, apple slices for us and two thermoses of water.

Finley ran down the walkway to the beach and bounded toward the water, whereupon he found a tennis ball. Leave it to Finley to find stuff. He brought his salty tennis ball to the wet sand above the tide line and proceeded to dig, flinging the sand and his ball backward, then retrieving the ball and dropping it into the hole that he excavated, only to start the sequence again. There were variations on this theme that I cannot even begin to describe. He had a wild look in his eye as he diligently played his new game, showing zero interest in engaging with possible playmates that were walking or running down the beach.

"C'mon, Finley, let's walk along the shore," I said. We saw Salt Island in the near distance; at low tide you can stroll out to the island, but this is not advisable unless you are immune to poison ivy. It covers the small island.

We had a wonderful view of the Twin Lights on Thatcher Island in the far distance. They are the only surviving multiple lights on the coasts of the United States and are some of the oldest lighthouses in the country.

Finley and I spent three and a half hours on Good Harbor Beach. It is easy to understand why this beach and its wonderful views were painted by Maurice Prendergast, Edward Hopper, and other artists. It is that gorgeous.

Finally, Finley and I left "dog heaven" and made our way over to the Eastern Point Lighthouse. Although the only road leading to it is marked "Private," we ignored the sign because the lighthouse is on Audubon property and access to it cannot be limited. We walked on the Dog Bar Breakwater leading out from the lighthouse and then sat on the flat rocks of the jetty where we saw the skyline of Boston on the western horizon. The sun was not due to set for another two hours, but we didn't stay for it.

"We will be back to see the sunset from this point," I told Finley as he was sitting by my side. "We should spend the night in nearby accommodations after you are allowed to return to the beach in October."

His tail happily wagged. He was in!

Finley is digging in the wet stand.

Finley is standing on the jetty in front of Eastern Point Lighthouse.

A Spring Romp at Gates Pond

April 15, 2021

🐾

"Dogs have mastered the art of living the good life. Every day is a glorious adventure. Every blade of grass is new and every squeak from their toy is as sweet-sounding as the last."
—Andrew Darrow, *Biscuit for Your Thoughts*

Walking the 2.4-mile loop trail around Gates Pond is one of my favorite walks in eastern Massachusetts. Finley does not have a favorite walk; one of the keys to his happiness is going for a romp in the countryside, any countryside. I once thought that I would take him to Manhattan to visit with my sister but quickly nixed the idea. He would be horrified by the ear-splitting sounds of the ambulance sirens, the blaring horns of the yellow taxis and the screeching noises of cars stopping just in time before hitting a jaywalker.

Finley is a country-born pup, and in the country, he lives his dream.

Located in Hudson and Berlin, Gates Pond is simply gorgeous. It is a perfect New England pond. There are no homes on it, although a hotel and dance hall once stood on its shores. A scattering of old stone walls line the wide, fairly flat loop trail. One site reviewer remarked, "You have to be pretty talented to get lost."

Finley and his recently neutered trail buddy, Tucker, were running together that morning; Tucker was especially happy to carouse with Finley because Tucker had finally been released from the week long restrictions following his surgery. It was no longer necessary for him to wear his postsurgical pajamas, fashionable though they were. Best of all, he could expend his energy off leash again. Free at last.

We reached a very small beach overlooking a small island in the pond. Finley swam close to shore while Tucker ventured into the water, stopping when it reached his ankles. The pond sparkled in the sunshine. My friend lobbed sticks into the water, giving Finley multiple opportunities to retrieve, while I took photographs. We found a cache of heavy-duty Finley sticks nearby. Obviously, other canines had availed themselves of the opportunity to cool off in the clear cool water of Gates Pond.

Tucker is crazy about Finley and in showing his excitement, leaped clear over him. To be sure, Finley loves Tucker, yet given the choice between Tucker and sticks, I think that Finley would choose the latter. Sorry, Tucker, but Finley is the quintessential "stick-o-maniac"!

The puppies occasionally left the water and returned to their humans to receive biscuits, which fueled their grand leisurely "exertions." We walked on, soon reaching the halfway point. More scenic views. Finley's yellow wiggle butt caught a ray of sunshine. "Forget the catwalk, strut your stuff on the dog walk," quips author Andrew Darrow.

There are certain mornings that one can designate as perfect. Today's was one of them.

Finley and Tucker enjoy Gates Pond together.

Finley found a waterlogged stick in Gates Pond.

A Beaver Dam on Hop Brook

April 22, 2021

🐾

No one appreciates the very special genius
of your conversation as your dog does.
—Christopher Morley, American journalist,
novelist, essayist, and poet

Finley was swimming about ten yards upstream from the big bridge spanning Hop Brook. Underneath the bridge was a beaver dam, a masterpiece of mud and sticks, stretching out across the brook for most of its width, here at the brook's narrowest section. There was a small breach on the opposite shore, allowing some water to tumble down the falls.

The dam caused much of the upstream water to back up, flooding the marsh and creating a lake of sorts. It provided the beavers with a perfect habitat to build their lodges.

Within minutes I heard the sound of heavy footsteps coming down the hill to my right. To my surprise, I saw a white bearded man, wearing waders and carrying a clam rake.

Had he missed the exit to Cape Cod? I thought. Afraid that he would not respond well to my inquiry, I complimented him on his nice looking waders. As if reading my mind, he told me that he is a specialist in the removal of beaver dams, which is necessary to stop the water from continued flooding and contamination of upstream wells and septic systems. This scenario is occurring throughout MA, with the exception of Cape Cod. In 1996, beaver trapping became illegal in our state, and the population has since exploded.

Finley had no hint of what was to come. Rick crossed the bridge and began the work of raking and removing the debris, the bulk of which consisted of large sticks. Finley took immediate notice. He swam over and looked hard at the man who was playing with sticks, Finley's sticks. Wanting to help, Finley began his own process of removing sticks from the dam. Perhaps he could join Rick's business, since Finley is a retriever par excellence? Perhaps he could be taught to remove sticks even faster? The problem, though, was that he was retrieving sticks from the upsteam side of the dam, which of course was on the wrong side.

The dam was four feet above grade, but Rick could only remove six inches of debris each day. If he removed much more than that, the rush of such a large amount of water would flood the road closest to Hop Brook.

When Rick finished his job, he told me that he loves Labradors and has raised them for twenty-five years. His chocolate and black Labs were waiting in his truck. "Can they come out to play with Finley?" I asked. Within minutes, Maeve and Bruin came running down the hill. Once they spotted Finley, a free-for-all ensued. Maeve, the five-year-old black Lab, is the mother of Bruin, the two-year-old chocolate Lab. When I saw them I thought of the logo of Labrador Retriever Rescue, a basket of three very young Lab puppies, one in each color.

And so here they were, one yellow, one chocolate and one black playing together, along the side of Hop Brook.

Finley looks at a man playing with sticks

Finley, Maeve, Bruin and Rick

A Visit to Baiting Brook-Welch Reservation

April 29, 2021

🐾

In a bygone era when twentieth-century Proper Bostonians mixed Beacon Hill formalities with country-side pleasures, Margaret Pearmain Welch (1893–1984) defied the mores of her social set and got away with it. She was the epitome of everything expected and much that was scandalous. Known as a debutante, dancer, world traveler, and hostess, she was also an indefatigable activist, writer, lecturer, lobbyist, fundraiser and opinion shaper. A descendant of 17th century dissenter Ann Hutchinson and just as independent, she embraced Quaker ideals of religious tolerance, conscientious objection and civil liberties, as well as worship without the benefit of clergy. She worked tirelessly on women's suffrage, reproductive rights, world peace, environmental protection, monetary reform, land conservation, and more.

—Elizabeth F. Fideler, *Margaret Pearmain Welch*

Once blocked from Callahan State Park by barbed wire, the trails of the Baiting Brook-Welch Reservation on the north side of the state park are now joined. Finley and I entered this tract at the edge of an agricultural field that once belonged to Penelope Turton, a pioneer in the development of organic farming in Massachusetts. I first heard about Penelope and her new farming methods in 1970, when my then post college roommate traveled to Penelope's Stearns Farm to study organic farming and join together with others to work in the fields. In return my friend received a bountiful box of organic vegetables and flowers. That was the beginning of the CSA (Community Supported Agriculture) movement.

Penelope Turton and Margaret Pearmain Welch were close friends. During the development boom following World War II, Margaret feared for her local landscape and donated eighty-seven acres of her land to the Sudbury Valley Trustees over a period of time, starting in 1959. The Welch gift eventually included five of the original ten acres of her feisty friend Penelope's farm land. The remaining five acres of Stearns Farm continue on in the tradition of CSA.

Finley and I walked past the fields and into the woods. A side path veered off into the right and Finley followed it. It was his day to decide on our route. He led me to a new find, the remains of a stone chimney whose hearth contained a lone cigarette butt. It was his first sniff of tobacco; I didn't catch the expression on his face but can only surmise he didn't care for it.

A short distance from the Baiting Brook-Welch Reservation, Finley and I drove through Barn Bridge, a covered bridge on Barnbridge Circle. Barn Bridge is on dry land and is not over anything. What an anomaly! We parked at the far end of the bridge and proceeded to sprint the length of its sixty-nine-foot span and then back again.

Such silliness.

Finley investigates the remains of a chimney.

Finley poses in front of Barn Bridge.

104

A Trip to Trap Falls in Ashby

May 6, 2021

It is bad to suppress laughter. It goes back
down and spreads to your hips.
—Fred Allen, comedian

Finley, we're going back to Trap Falls! Do you remember when we were there in mid-October when the falls were a mere trickle? I promised you then that we would return in the spring when the falls would be thundering over the ledges. That's a sure thing now that it's mid-April.

Trap Falls is located in a very picturesque setting in the Willard Brook State Forest in Ashby. The falls consist of two side by side "plunges." There are six distinguishable types of waterfalls in New England: fan, horsetail, cascade, punch bowl, block, and plunge.

Each waterfall is rated on a scale of 1–5 stars depending on how impressive or scenic the fall is. Size does not matter. Trap Falls rates four and a half stars on the scale. As a plunge waterfall, Trap Falls flows over a rim and drops at an entirely vertical angle.

After I parked our car, Finley and I reached the falls in about five minutes. He jumped into a pool of water about fifty yards downstream. As he became more acclimated, he swam back to shore, ran up the path closer to the plunges and dared to jump in. How he found a stick in the churning water, I'll never know. We had the waterfall to ourselves that morning, which was an additional treat.

An hour passed. Two women suddenly appeared; I say "suddenly," because we didn't hear them above the crashing sound of the falls. They laughed when they saw determined Finley swimming out to retrieve sticks. The women began throwing sticks out into the water, and by noon more people began to arrive. Some of them began to set out their lunches on the nearby picnic tables while the children came closer to shore, naturally drawn to Finley and his playfulness. Some of them hooted in delight. Finley kept a partial eye on them and beamed. Due to his exertions, Finley's red harness tore into two pieces and was left hanging on his body. We stayed for another hour and were reluctant to leave, but part two of today's adventure was waiting for us. Finley kept looking back as we made our way to the parking lot.

Next, we visited Jewel Hill (elevation 1,409 feet), the newest property of The Trustees of Reservation and now open to the public. As the car climbed up toward the property, we began to see snow. Soon, panoramic views of Mt. Wachusett appeared on the horizon.

A 0.7 mile trail on Jewel Hill leads to the Hudson Overlook, where on a clear day you can see the Boston skyline forty-five miles away. Jewel Hill's 496-acre landscape is known locally as Crocker Farm, after the family that owned and operated the dairy farm here through most of the postwar twentieth century.

It's a given that Finley had plenty of energy left for exploration during the remainder of the afternoon. He played in the meadows, the forest and even met a six-month-old black Lab named Daisy.

Finley and I had a superb day together. Laughter, love and adventures, all rolled into one.

Finley is running in the meadows at Jewel Hill

Finley inhales the spring air at Trap Falls

On the Ghost Trail and Beyond

May 13, 2021

🐾

Considering that at the heart of most rumored hauntings is a tragic and mysterious story, it's little wonder that they intrigue us so much. Though skeptics may chuckle, the mystery of things that go bump in the night seem to hold a unique appeal for believers and non-believers.

—*New England Today TRAVEL*

It is fairly unusual that Finley and I venture out for a walk in the forest before sunset, but my sudden intuition led us out to the Nobscot Boy Scout Reservation. Because Finley's facial expression is often one of positive expectancy, with the exception of his weekly tooth-brushing sessions, I didn't ask him if he wanted to join me. His attitude is "Yo voy contigo" (I go with you). He knows a little Spanish.

We decided to set our course for the Ghost Trail, possibly an interesting walk to take in the waning hours of this spring day.

"Let's tune in, Finley," I said as we turned left onto the trail.

Is its name referring to an actual ghost that haunts this specific area, or is it a tall tale told by a scout leader to kids who love to be scared while sitting around the campfire? Nothing out of the ordinary occurred as we walked the short Ghost Trail. After leaving the trail and as luck would have it, we came across a woman and her dog. She told me that recently her dog was spooked while walking on the Ghost Trail and that he ran off into the woods, his tail between his legs. She repeatedly called out to him to return, though it took a while for him to do so. She had never seen her dog act like this before. While we talked, Finley and his pal ran around in happy circles.

The next morning Finley and I returned to the reservation looking for answers. We passed the remote scout family pavilion where Finley and I played a game of retrieving a tennis ball from the tops of different picnic tables. We continued down the path and came to a smallish gap in the stone wall on our right; set back in the woods was the Nobscot Smallpox Cemetery. According to Framingham and Sudbury historical records, in the late 1700s the towns of Framingham and Sudbury buried their dead from a smallpox epidemic "as far away from the town centre as possible," because smallpox is contagious. The infected were quarantined in a nearby "pest house." About one-third of those infected died and were buried with no grave markers. Finley investigated the area which consists of rocks that mark the graves. The graves were sad to see.

But the burial ground is a good distance from the Ghost Trail, and since ghosts are tied to the location of their deaths, it is reasonable to assume that there is no connection between the burial ground and the trail.

What about the Native American populations that once lived in this area? We know that they were ravaged by the white settlers who stole their lands, etc. Could those deceased Native Americans or white settlers, or both, have produced a spirit that didn't know it was dead and that remained attached to this plane of consciousness?

Lee Swanson, the former head of the Sudbury Historical Society, and local historian Yan-Jan Hardenbergh both told me that they are unaware of any ghostly activity reported on the reservation.

Does that mean that the question has been settled? Probably not. Perhaps Finley, who lives entirely in his senses, has a clue. His forest pal likely did perceive something out of the ordinary.

Finley explores the Nobscot Smallpox Cemetery.

Finley stares at a tennis ball before retrieving it.

Looking Back on All the Fun

May 20, 2021

🐾

The affection both ways is unalterably tender. Teddy sits on the couch next to me and gingerly places his paw on my shoulder. The Beatles sang, "The love you take is equal to the love you make." Not true in our dog universe. I can't come close to giving as much as I get from Teddy.
—Diana Nyad, the first person to swim without the aid of a shark cage from Cuba to Florida

It's been my mission through my column to tell you about the fun-filled adventures of a free-spirited yellow Labrador retriever named Finley. On the first anniversary of the publication of his column, it's time to stop and look back at a few of the stories.

Near the beginning of his adventures, he met a potbelly pig named Sgt. Schultz, a blue roan horse named Prairie, and a flock of sheep that lived on a farm in Ashby. Finley has taken flying leaps off steep embankments in order to retrieve all manner of sticks; he even tried to remove a stick that served as the arm of a snow woman who was sitting on a frozen lake in the dead of winter. He has walked the green space of the abandoned rail bed that Protect Sudbury is trying to safeguard against the alarming plans of Eversource.

Finley has explored the Glacial Features Walk at the Gray Reservation. He has journeyed to southern New Hampshire where he swam in a pond that mirrored Mount Monadnock, the second most climbed mountain on earth. His first trip to Vermont saw him swimming in Lake Champlain, summiting his first mountain, and carousing with Bo, another yellow Lab puppy half his age. Finley spent five mostly foggy days on a beach in Goose Rocks, Maine. He had a blast.

On other occasions, he visited a spa and weeks later relaxed on a blanket in the grass while receiving a massage specifically designed for the canine set. Finley once found a rubber ducky floating down Hop Brook; on the same day he followed his nose to a tepee where he discovered a teenage couple who lay sleeping. Oops!

Finley has explored Gloucester's Good Harbor Beach in the off season. His broad chest, strong limbs and otter tail make it possible for him to swim and run for hours. On one lazy summer afternoon he swam in Stiles Pond in Spencer where he rocked my kayak while attempting to hoist himself into it. We were about twenty yards from shore.

Finley has visited the King Philip Woods where he found an old tire and a submerged soccer ball. He sat by my side at the Haynes Garrison House where I told him the story of the Sudbury Fight. Of course Finley has explored some

Finley relishes being at Good Harbor Beach

of Thoreau's old haunts; in October he swam in Sudbury River's Fairhaven Bay, and on the ledge of the historic stone boathouse, he quietly watched the colorful leaves as they rustled in the autumn breezes. He sat in a canoe as we paddled under the North Bridge in Concord and was given permission to jump out of the canoe when we reached Egg Rock, the meeting point of our three rivers: the Sudbury River, the Assabet River and the Concord River.

Finley visited Ponyhenge, a graveyard of abandoned rocking horses, and by mere chance discovered its backstory. Nearby and on the same adventure, I bought Finley a Whoofie Pie, which he refused to eat, from the Whoopie Wagon. No refunds were allowed.

In October, Finley donned his new Super Dog costume and visited/kissed the little girls next door who were also decked out in their Halloween best.

When we went forest bathing, Finley climbed into my lap and together, with all of our senses alive, felt what nature provided. What gifts! No wonder I love him so much.

Thanks, Finley, for being my fun-loving companion and mentor always ready to head out, no matter the weather. I feel privileged to have you in my life. A toast to many more years of adventures together, Finley!

A Visit to Delaney Pond

May 27, 2021

> Since we now know for sure that every dog is really listening when we talk, there's every reason to continue lavishing attention on our pups, both linguistically and otherwise. And when you train, make sure to use clear command words, to make it as easy as possible for your pup to understand. After all, they're the ones doing most of the work here: humans have not learned any words in Doggish.
>
> —American Kennel Club

Before Finley and I reached Hank the puppy, a mixture of bloodhound and pit bull, his father called out to us, "It's his first birthday today!" I thought that I was the only nut that announced these kinds of things to strangers. I had met a kindred soul.

Finley dashed off to greet Hank; within seconds they began to run together, doing what outgoing puppies do. Hank's dad began to tell me about the birthday party planned for later that day. Many of the neighborhood dogs were invited to the party; most of them were adopted during the past fifteen months, a direct result of the pandemic. Dog biscuits and beer would be served. I switched topics and asked him to tell me about the bloodhound part of his puppy.

"Well," he said, "Hank will spend twenty minutes at a time, nose to the ground, following an ant across the patio. That is one of his favorite activities. The ants should relocate."

I should mention that Finley and I were walking on an earthen dam overlooking Delaney Pond, a medium size pond located in Bolton, Harvard and Stow. As part of the Delaney Complex and lying at the center of the property, Delaney Pond provides a habitat for otter, fisher and many bird and fish species. It is also a good site for butterflies and migratory waterfowl. The 397-acre complex serves three purposes: two dams provide flood control; a wildlife conservation area surrounds the pond; and there is access to recreation, such as walking, boating, fishing and hunting.

On this southern section of the pond, we had expansive views of grassland that likely had once been a farmstead. Finley and I followed the path up to the western side of the pond and soon made our way down to the water. We saw a couple of swans in the distance. In a couple of minutes, two honking geese flew directly over us. Finley looked up, tracing the geese across the sky while I resisted the urge to take photos, at least for now. Though I can't say why, Finley and I left this blissful spot and rejoined the trail. We passed by sections of cattail marshes and entered the woods. I had read that many people had gotten lost in these wood due to the crisscross trails.

"C'mon, Finley, let's get out of the woods; let's head back to the wide-open spaces." He followed me back into the sunshine of the day.

Before we reached the parking lot, I saw two women walking toward us. With broad smiles, they were evidently taking pleasure in watching Finley have an absolutely grand time. As they passed I heard one of them say to the other, "He looks so happy!"

Finley and Hank are enjoying Delaney Pond

Finley is standing in the pond

Finley and Bo Visit the deCordova Sculpture Park

June 3, 2021

🐾

The deCordova is internationally recognized as a major venue for the exhibition and interpretation of modern and contemporary outdoor sculpture. The Sculpture Park occupies 30 acres of beautifully landscaped lawns, forests, gardens and terraces on a rolling site along the shore of Flint's Pond. At any given time, approximately 60 sculptures are on display at the Sculpture Park.

—the trustees.org

"Finley, Bo's back in town and boy do we have great plans," I said, as our Connecticut friends turned into the driveway. I didn't want to tell him in advance of their visit, so as not to unnecessarily excite him. He heard them pull in and rocketed out of his chair, begging to go outside and give them a proper Labrador welcome. "Wait five seconds, Finley," I told him, sensitive to his cries of impatience.

Finley and his friend Bo, a one-year-old yellow Lab pup, greeted one another by tumbling, rolling and running on the grass together, exactly as one would expect. Although Bo's parents and I had visited the Sculpture Park on numerous occasions, Finley and Bo had not. As we entered the park, we could see the bucolic landscape spread out before us; a handful of people strolled the grounds. Finley and Bo delighted in playing beneath the boughs of an ancient beech tree. They ran down to Flint's Pond for a short swim. They drank water and ate dog biscuits as we sat beside Eve Celebrant, Marianna Pineda's large bronze sculpture, now oxidized to a beautiful shade of turquoise. The piece is described as "a powerful and graceful tribute to womanhood." It is simply gorgeous.

Although the color red is not a part of Finley and Bo's visual spectrum, they sat in front of Heavy Handed, a bright red larger than life sculpture by Nathan Mabry. The piece is a hand gesture that to some represents a peace sign, for others a victory sign. The pups were happy to please me when I asked them to sit within the sculpture Rain Gates by Ron Rudnicki. It is a pleasing granite sculpture set at the edge of the woods. That afternoon stroll with Finley and Bo was unique and relaxing.

We didn't have time to take the long walk around Flint's Pond. We will do this in October because I want to show Finley a special grove of white birch trees whose leaves turn bright yellow in autumn.

Picture the following: yellow Finley stands in the foreground with his red collar; white birch trees with their yellow leaves serve as the middle ground, and a deep-blue sky graces the background. I can't wait to take that picture.

"Raingate" **"Heavy handed"**

Celebrating Prairie's Special Day

June 10, 2021

🐾

Instructions for living a life: Pay attention.
Be astonished. Tell about it.
—Mary Oliver, Pulitzer Prize-winning poet (1935–2019)

I had partially kept my promise to Prairie: Finley and I would visit with her for at least an hour every other day, poor weather notwithstanding. Yet, after only two visits, it became clear that Finley could not continue to spend time with her. Their initial nose to nose greetings were followed by Finley rushing around her paddock searching for partially desiccated road apples for his afternoon snack. His visits came to an abrupt halt.

Now many months later, I learned that Prairie was going to turn sixteen in a couple of weeks. Why not celebrate this special day by having a Sweet Sixteen party for her?

After hearing my proposal, Dotti, Prairie's no-nonsense parent, declared, "I have a party hat that she can wear."

"And I'll bring Finley (for old time's sake) and a carrot cake for the party," I announced. I reasoned that because Prairie loves carrots and sweets, a carrot cake would not be a big stretch for her.

Horses and dogs mature at a much faster rate than humans. For example, a human child can take over a year to learn to walk, while a horse will walk an hour after birth. At sixteen years of age, Prairie would be fifty and a half years old in human years. Pixie, Prairie's new paddock mate, an eight-year-old pinto pony mare and half of Prairie's height, would be coming to the party as well.

At 5:30 p.m. May 16, Finley and I pulled into Dutton Downs, the horse farm that serves as Prairie's home. Finley was excited to be back; his tail wagged and his nose twitched as he inhaled the familiar barn smells. Dotti and her husband Paul led Prairie and Pixie out from their pen to a large swath of grass in front of their house. They looked so adorable together! The P&P girls began mowing swaths of spring grass, eating quickly and with great pleasure. Dotti attempted to place the party hat on Prairie's fair head, but Dotti ended up wearing the hat instead. We sang the happy birthday song to Prairie. Finley was thrilled, thinking the song was meant for him. Smart as he is, he didn't comprehend that a horse could also be a beneficiary of the birthday song.

As for the carrot cake, Prairie sniffed it and turned away; she returned to eating her preferred grass. Paul took a piece of the cake and held it under her nose, trying to persuade her to have the bite, but it was not meant to be. Instead the cake fell to the ground right where Finley was standing/waiting, and without a pause he gobbled it up.

We were a mix of three species on that lovely afternoon, and in our own way and together, we had a blast.

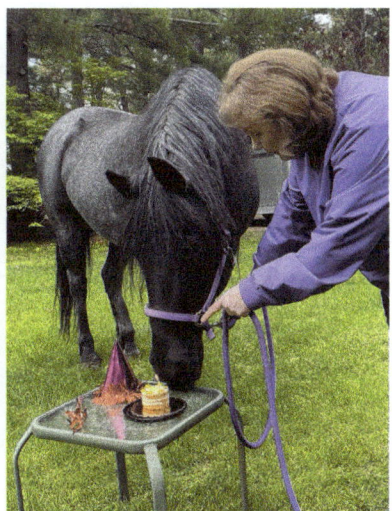

Party animals

Prairie sniffs her birthday cake.

Savoring a sunset and barking at a leopard

Finley frolics at sunset. **Finley is watching PBS.**

Finley Savors a Sunset and Barks at a Leopard

June 17, 2021

🐾

There are specific factors that are common to canine aggression. The types of aggression include dominance aggression, defensive aggression and maternal aggression. Aggression in canines may be a self-defense response to a person or animal entering a dog's space.

—Wikipedia

When I think of a landscape filled with open fields, woodlands and a picturesque pond, I think of taking Finley to Callahan State Park. We walk its trails in the winter, spring and fall, skipping the summer because at that time of year Eagle Pond becomes a breeding ground for the bacteria that can cause canine eye infections.

Finley and I had not experienced a sunset at the park until two days ago. Sunny skies with some passing cumulus clouds blended together to provide us with an opportunity to view a very colorful sunset that day.

"Finley, let's go to Callahan and share a sunset together," I proclaimed when I saw that the sky remained perfect for our outing.

At 7:00 p.m., we started our walk along the earthen dam at Callahan. We had an hour and fifteen minutes to do as we pleased: to walk, run or contemplate the vagaries of life. Naturally, Finley found a playmate while I sat on a lone bench facing west.

Eventually the sky became illuminated with gorgeous pink parallel lines that veered north. Somehow it seemed that Finley became aware of the sky and he came running up the embankment to sit by my side. I have found that most sunset watchers leave their positions at the point of sundown, some even cheer. Finley and I remained for another twenty minutes basking in the intense red afterglow. Two deer were running in the field behind us, but Finley didn't notice.

When night settled in, Finley had another adventure, but this one was not to his liking. We sat comfortably together on our chair and a half when I started to play the PBS *Nature* episode about African leopards. The narrator described leopards as "marvels of necessity, killing to live." Finley is an excellent watch dog, a predator in his own right, but he might be placated with a tasty biscuit if a human predator broke into our house.

When Finley is awakened by animal sounds coming from the television, he sits up and takes notice. His tail wags hard when he sees the dogs perform in the Subaru commercials. But Finley had never before seen a ferocious leopard in action. He watched as the leopard plucked a stork out of the sky; ominous music ratcheted up his tension. This was a distinct violation of his space, a huge threat to him. Roaring his upset, he kicked off the chair and a half. Then he discerned the leopard slinking behind a bush. Finley was beyond comforting. With a quick click of the TV remote control, I made the leopard disappear. Finley climbed into my lap, his heart still thumping.

When I watch the remainder of the show, I will ban Finley from the room though I will miss his large lapdog warmth, no matter the season.

Finley Visits the Historic Wayside Inn in Sudbury

June 24, 2021

Finley had never been to the Wayside Inn before. We arranged a personal tour of the property with Steve Pickford, the innkeeper of the Wayside Inn, and Sally Purrington Hild, the director of the nonprofit Wayside Inn Foundation.

In the pastoral countryside of Sudbury, Massachusetts, sits a charming relic of the colonial past. Having begun as a modest two-room family residence in 1707, and officially becoming a working inn in 1716, Longfellow's Wayside Inn has survived and flourished in its nearly 300 years of hosting guests and travelers.

—*New England Today*

Finley had never been to the Wayside Inn before. We arranged a personal tour of the property with Steve Pickford, the innkeeper of the Wayside Inn, and Sally Purrington Hild, the director of the nonprofit Wayside Inn Foundation.

By 10:00 a.m., the temperature had reached into the low eighties, and I knew that Finley's happiness would depend upon drenching himself in the nearest pond or stream. But I am getting ahead of myself. While we three humans were walking and talking, Finley sat in the shade at stops along the way.

I had always assumed that Sudbury residents as well as residents in neighboring towns were used to walking the paths of the Wayside Inn complex. There are nine historic structures and features in the complex, including a stone grist mill, a cider house, the Carding Mill Pond and the Red Stone schoolhouse, affectionately known as the Little Red Schoolhouse, where Mary took her sickly lamb to school one day in 1815. This true story became famous when the nursery rhyme, "Mary Had a Little Lamb" was published.

In answer to my assumption that visitors were familiar with the complex, Sally assured me that such was not the case. "The majority of guests come only to dine at the inn and do not tour the rest of the property," she replied. While we walked, I asked my two hosts to tell me a little bit about their work at the inn. One aspect of Sally's mission is to provide educational programming for adults and children. Weekly Strawberry Summer Concerts are held at the chapel beginning on July 2. There are six Eat, Drink, and Be Merry events held each year and numerous other programs for adults. Some children's events include story walks and crafts programs.

During his eight years as the innkeeper, Steve developed the inn's newest trail, the Innkeeper's Loop, a lovely perimeter trail that we walked. Steve pointed out the many chestnut and apple trees that were planted throughout the property.

When Ezekiel Howe took over his father's tavern, Howe's Tavern, in 1744, he changed its name to The Red Horse Tavern. The sign of a red horse was placed at the inn's entryway, which indicated the location of the inn to the many people who could not read or write. The inn became famous when Henry Wadsworth Longfellow employed it as a setting for his book of poetry *Tales of a Wayside Inn* in 1863. Had it not been for Longfellow, the old inn would never have come to the attention of Henry Ford, the billionaire auto magnate who purchased the property in 1923. He restored the inn and its land to its former serene beauty and added the nine outbuildings. Due to Henry Ford's redemption, the inn blossomed. It is now the oldest operating inn in the United States.

By this time Finley had stopped listening and was ready for a dunk in Hop Brook. Afterward, and before I could re-leash him, he sped toward the outdoor tables on the right side of the inn where guests were having lunch. He ran around the tables eliciting much surprise. Horrified, I quickly looked around and heard people laughing in amusement. We were lucky that day.

So it goes with Finley and his many adventures.

A Visit to Peach Hill and the Nashoba Valley Winery

July 1, 2021

🐾

Since first producing fruit wines in 1978, the family-owned Nashoba Valley Winery, located in the heart of Massachusetts' apple country, is set on a 52-acre stunning hilltop orchard and winery.

— Nashoba Valley Winery brochure

The Peach Hill Conservation area in Berlin (emphasis on the first syllable), a partnership between the town's Conservation Commission and the Sudbury Valley Trustees, opened to the public last summer. The collaboration gives SVT a conservation restriction on the property, administering the preservation of its outstanding natural features and wildlife. Improving the trails, creating trail maps and building bridges over stream crossings are also part of its mission.

On the morning of June 10, Finley and I journeyed to Peach Hill to meet Mark Sykes, the SVT steward of the property; he was going to give us a personal tour. The Mountain Laurel Trail is the main trail at Peach Hill, and I knew that these gorgeous flowers would be blooming during the first two weeks in June.

We entered a lovely upland forest of mixed hardwoods and pine. Large glacial erratics strewn about by the last glacier were prominent as we began our hike. What a grand entrance it was! Finley sized up the erratics and realized that he couldn't climb any of them, although in past days he was able to climb up smaller erratics, especially if he spotted a stick on the top.

Within minutes, we began to see thick stands of Mountain Laurel in full bloom. Some of the stands were an impressive ten feet tall; the white color of these blossoms stood out against the dark green color of the woods.

Finley is standing in a dangerous pond.

Finley, as usual, jumped for joy as he explored his new playground. The trail ended at Wattaquadock Pond, and Finley raced down the path to go swimming, part of his morning constitutional. We saw a large area of water lilies; their large yellow buds would be blooming in a week or two. While Finley swam, Mark spoke of the number of bobcat and black bear sightings in these woods and also the nearby Forty Caves Reservation.

The Peach Hill Conservation area is likely named after the many surrounding fruit orchards where strawberries, peaches, nectarines, apples and other fruits are grown.

For part two of the day's adventure, we drove to the just-down-the-road to the Nashoba Valley Winery where I intended to buy a bottle of peach wine. By the way, peach wine pairs beautifully with ginger biscuits or snaps. There were a tiny number of winery visitors that day. When Finley saw a young saleswoman standing by the door to the winery building, he flashed her a smile and was promptly invited to come in. I hope that she didn't mind that I tagged along.

A small pond was set in front of the winery building, and for the second time that day, Finley dashed in for a short swim. Suddenly, a woman appeared by my side and said, "Do you know that this pond is infested with leeches and snapping turtles?" Upset by hearing the news, I lowered my voice and commanded Finley to leave the pond immediately. I subsequently learned that these particular leeches can grow to five inches in length!

When Finley came ashore, I examined every inch of him for any evidence of bloodthirsty leeches. There were none. Now it was time to go home. Nestled in the backseat of our car, he snoozed on the ride back.

All was right and good with Finley on his action-packed day.

Some Previously Unpublished Photos

July 8, 2021

🐾

I am having a quiet staycation this week. Instead of portraying a Finley adventure this week, I am sending you, dear readers, four Finley unpublished photos that I hope you like.

Happy trails,
Sherry

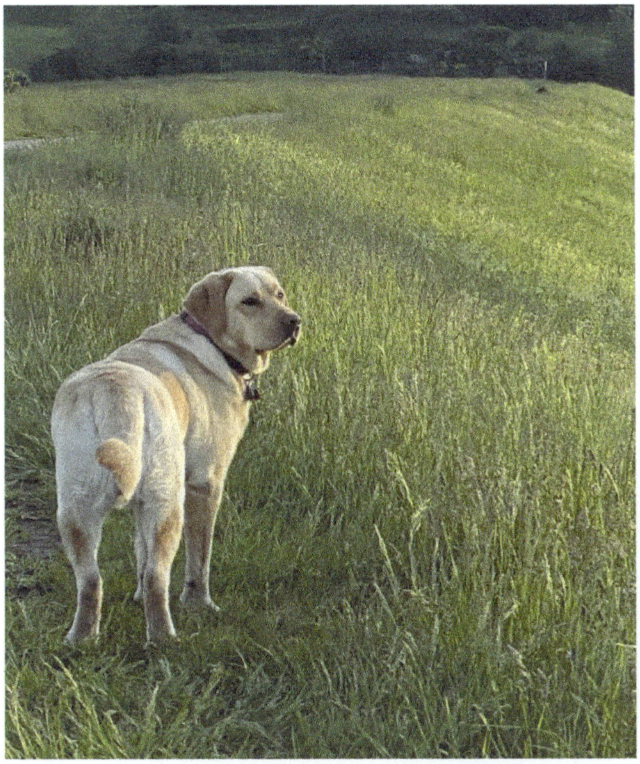
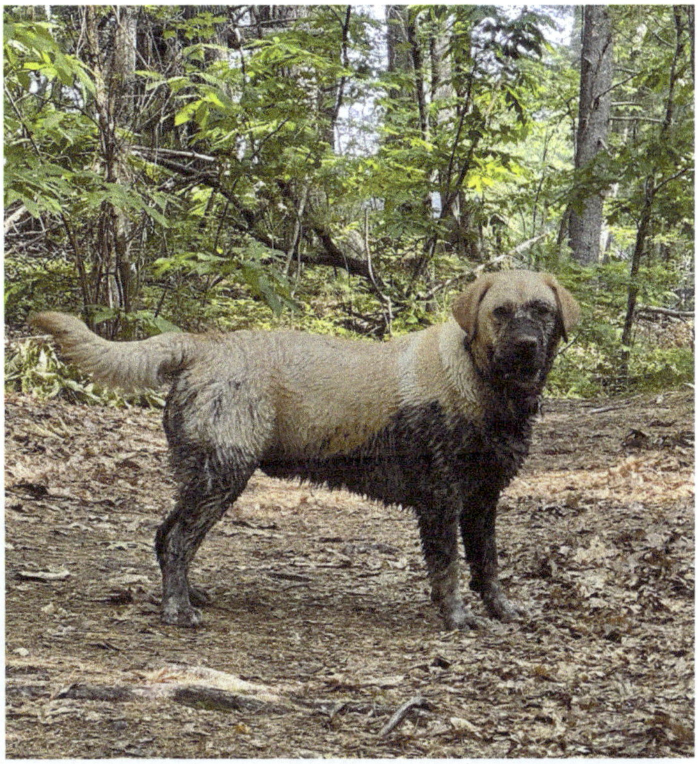
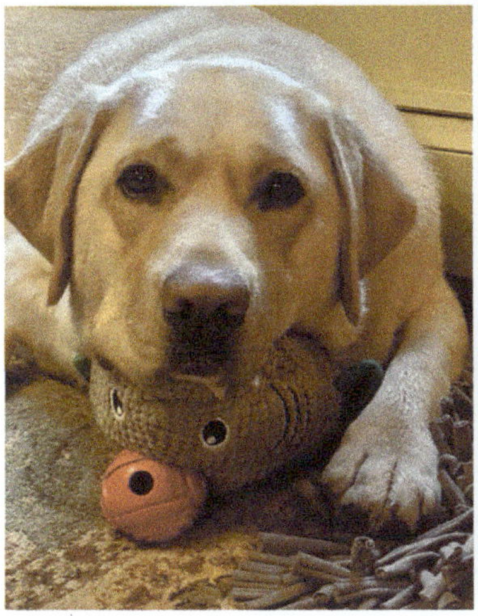
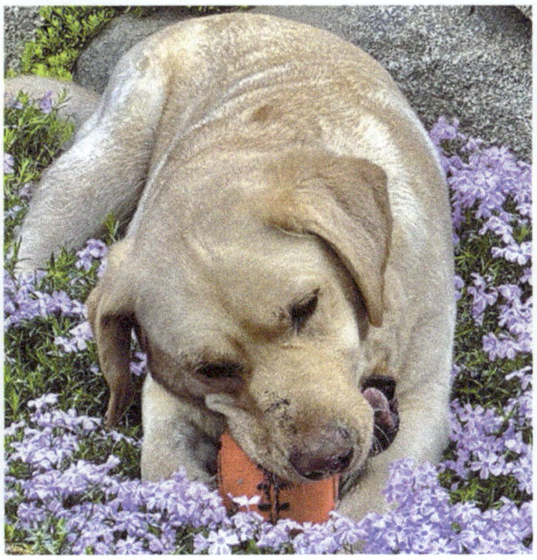
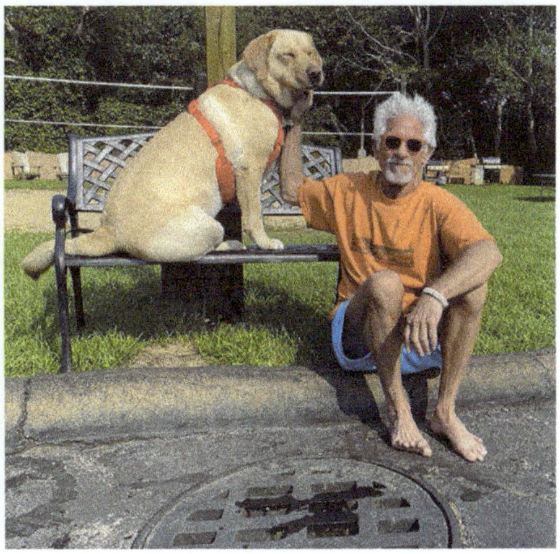

A Walk after the Rain

July 22, 2021

🐾

    Dogs have already proven their ability to sniff out diseases ranging from cancer to malaria. While we don't always know exactly what they are detecting to ferret out specific illnesses, the clues are likely tied to a dog's ability to smell volatile organic compounds—the metabolic junk our bodies produce all the time, which can vary with illness. With 220 million scent receptors, versus the 5 million scent receptors that humans have, they can sniff substances that are diluted to a point of just one part per trillion, or the equivalent of smelling one drop of liquid in the combined volume of 20 Olympic swimming pools.

—Dogster

My rain gauge, measuring five inches of rain, has filled and refilled a few times in the first three weeks following the summer solstice. There are giant puddles in the woods reflecting the trees above and providing wonderful opportunities for abstract photography. Generally I wear ankle high rubber boots in the woods when there has been a lot of rain, but now to be on the safe side, I sometimes wear my tall Wellies. Global warming charts have already predicted a warmer and wetter climate for our region. And so it has come to pass.

Finley, being a Lab, of course, has a sense of smell that is very keen; it may be up to a million times greater than our own. So the muck and mud smells resulting from our significant rainfall has caused him to be more crazily excited than usual. As if that's even possible! Running through puddles and leaping into swollen streams while his great schnoz works overtime, has been Finley's greatest pleasure lately.

In the summer, Dudley Brook is a slow-moving stream. Now, it runs with the force of a big snowmelt on an April day. Finley was standing in Dudley Brook on one morning last week when a large stick rushing along in the current became lodged in his collar. He didn't notice it. He just strode to the far side of the stream to smell more decaying vegetation. When he eventually came ashore, I tried to remove the stick from his collar, but my boots slid and I slipped and fell backward into the deep mud. As I lay there unhurt, I started to laugh. Finley, thinking that this was a new game, jumped over my face, flinging mud and water all over me. Wet muddy Finley, wet muddy me.

A day in the life, oh boy!

Finley savors the July rain.

A stick is lodged in Finley's collar.

126

Hop Brook

July 29, 2021

🐾

Blue-green algae is a bacteria that lives in freshwater and often lives in colonies large enough to be visible to the naked eye. Its growth can be spurred by the phosphorus and nitrogen-rich nutrients that can be found in runoffs from farms, towns and suburbs, especially those found in shallow, warm stretches of warm water. Blue-green algae (Cyanobacteria) can be deadly to animals if they ingest infected water while swimming or playing in it.

—*USA Today*, **July 15, 2021.**

I've been reading about the sudden proliferation of blue-green algae blooms in our area. The heavy rains of early summer have caused the runoff of fertilizers and other farm and garden chemicals into our lakes and ponds. As a result, there has been a development and expansion of these toxic blooms which look bluish green or the colors of green pea soup or turquoise paint. Lake Cochituate and White Pond beaches, just to name a couple of them, are closed to swimmers.

Blue-green algae is always present in our lakes and ponds, but I've never seen anything that approaches the number of algae mats that in some cases completely cover the surface of the water.

Finley must be leashed before we approach these infected waters, but he doesn't understand why. His eyes usually question me: *How come, Mom?*

For the last few weeks, Finley has been swimming in the fast water below the waterfall at Hop Brook. Yesterday he ran down the steep slope to the brook and leaped in, while I held onto a tree for balance. How he found an old pylon remains a mystery; all I know is that he climbed up the embankment to show off his once-in-a-lifetime find. Finley loves salmon treats, and I attempted to trade one of them for his dirty and disgusting discovery. No trade! To distract him, I hurled a nice, juicy stick downstream. Finley swam forcefully, gaining on the stick until he captured it. Then I threw another stick upstream; he barreled through the water, taking account of the position of the stick in the current as it crazily moved downstream. Good boy Finley was able to retrieve it.

I sidestepped for a few dozen feet to get closer to the falls. For Finley's final challenge I threw a large stick into the whitewater that was churning at the bottom of the falls. No matter his strength and perseverance, he lost sight of it. Then I found another Finley stick and again threw it downstream. It was, by now, an easy retrieval for him. I wanted to finish his play/exercise session on a good note.

Afterward, we drove over to the local pet shop. Today was July 18, National Ice Cream Day, so we ventured in only to learn that corporate headquarters hadn't informed its local employees of its advertised sundae bar for canines! The manager made good on the promise and gave Finley a tub of Wag More Bark Less, human-grade, dairy-free peanut butter ice cream with probiotics. Finley swallowed a scoop of it and was thrilled.

Finley continued to smile as we walked the short distance back to our car.

For the last few weeks, Finley has been swimming in the fast water below the waterfall at Hop Brook.

A Lazy Trip Down the Sudbury River

August 5, 2021

🐾

The profile of a river bed determines how fast it flows. The Sudbury River's overall gradient is 5 feet per mile. The river does nearly all its falling in its first 16 miles. The lower half is nearly level, dropping only a matter of inches. At flood stage, water pouring from the Assabet River causes the Sudbury to flow backwards.

—**Ron McAdow,** *The Concord, Sudbury, and Assabet Rivers*

We formed a flotilla of two boats on that splendid afternoon in late June: a forest-green canoe and one yellow kayak. Finley had much loved his maiden voyage paddling down the Sudbury and Concord rivers last October, so I knew that he would continue to do well as we set out for an adventure through the Great Meadows National Wildlife section of the Sudbury River. The river flows for 31.2 miles until it joins the Assabet River at Egg Rock. We launched our boats and paddled up river through an area known as Sedge Meadows (mile marker 22.9) for the stands of Tussock Sedges lining both sides of the river. Finley positioned himself squarely in the middle of the canoe, his bright orange life jacket worn to save his life should the boat tip over. Goodness knows why I put the jacket on him. If swamped, Finley could easily swim to shore and back again and back again almost endlessly. On the other hand, Finley's life jacket would indeed save his life if he were to fall off of a sailboat five miles from shore unbeknownst to his family and friends. Heaven forbid.

The rough, triangular sedges rose to a height of three feet. Finley listened to the lively songs of red-winged blackbirds and marsh wrens. He saw the pterodactyl-like great blue heron that was wading along the edge, hopscotching down the river if we got too close to it. We paddled up to Stone's Bridge by the golf course at the Wayland Country Club. A few dozen yards inland from the river stands a stone marker commemorating the citizens of Concord who died helping those of Wayland and Sudbury during the King Philip's War. Had I known of its existence prior to today's paddle, we might have left our boats and walked in to pay our respects.

It was now snack time and we drew our boats in to be closer together. Though Finley prefers sticks and balls to most edibles, he gobbled down his snack in two seconds flat.

Needless to say, Finley enjoyed being paddled down our lazy summer river. Reluctant to leave the water, he just sat in the canoe and had to be coaxed to jump out onto dry land. My fab Lab.

Finley is seated in a canoe in the middle of the Sudbury River.

Finley looks out as he approaches Stone's Bridge in Wayland

Visiting Dog Beach in Nahant

August 12, 2021

🐾

I am mesmerized by the sea. The ebb and flow of waves coming in, moving back is like the breathing rhythm of the universe. I find deep peace in merging with it and happy to be lost in it.

—Dr. Steve Isenberg

If you are a canine parent, you might want to know that Dog Beach in Nahant, on the north shore of Massachusetts, is an important find because you are allowed to take your unleashed pooch there throughout the year. The beach is located off the causeway connecting the city of Lynn and the town of Nahant, the latter having a land area of only one square mile and making it the smallest municipality in the state.

A hard rain fell on that Sunday morning in late July. Finley and I were due to go for a walk on Dog Beach, and so when it stopped raining by early afternoon, we set out on our sixty-five-minute drive to meet our friend Steve. He recently moved from Sudbury to the coastal town of Marblehead where he grew up. He told us that he "longed to breathe the salt air and feel the wide-open spaces of the beaches."

The tide was out when we arrived. A few people and dogs were walking on the hard packed sand. With Nahant Bay located on one side of the causeway and the open ocean on the other side, breezes/winds are often present.

We reached the entryway to the beach. Finley made a mad dash for the water before I could throw his bouncy rubber ball toward the ocean. He reached the ocean and stopped. With mounting tension Finley looked in my direction, waiting for me to launch the ball. I threw it relatively far now that the muscles in my right arm are slightly more developed, a result of throwing balls and sticks to Finley since he was a little pup. Thank you, Finley!

Finley spotted them first. Standing on their boards were two surfers in wetsuits moving toward shore. How could this be? The waves were almost nonexistent. As is his way, Finley swam out to greet the surfers and retrieve one of their boards. We all laughed. To divert Finley's attention, one of the surfers encouraged him to mount the blue surfboard. Finley's first surfing lesson! He hoisted himself up onto the board and slid off the other side. Another round of laughter. Two more attempts were made with similar results.

The 2021 Dog Surfing Championship recently took place in the UK. Small dogs and their owners surfed together; I saw photos of the small dogs firmly planted on the front of the boards. Now imagine lumbering Finley having mastered the art of sticking to a surfboard and catapulting his human surfer right onto the beach!

We walked for another twenty minutes or so while Finley ran up and down the beach and in and out of the ocean. Always in pursuit of pleasure, dear Finley tapped into the sounds of children playing down the beach.

I loudly called out to them, "He's F–R–I–E–N–D–L–Y; if you want to play with him, run into the water!" That's how the game of chase began.

"Finley," I told him as we headed home to forested Sudbury, "it's all about our great adventures, our growth and where to go next."

He nodded, ever so slightly.

Finley is trying to mount a surfboard.

Finley is having fun in the ocean.

Finding Places to Cool Off

August 19, 2021

🐾

In the summertime when the weather is hot, you
can stretch right up and touch the sky.
—Ray Dorset, "In the Summertime"

Boon Lake beach in Stowe has just been added to the list of lakes and ponds affected by the larger-than-normal presence of blue-green algae, making it dangerous for swimming. Eagle Pond in Callahan State Park has thus far been unaffected by the proliferation of this bacteria, so we set our sights for an early morning romp to this magnificent park.

It was going to be a hot, sunny day. Finley ran ahead of me, greeting dogs along the way. He turned a corner and reached the pond first. When I got closer, I could see him swimming around with an energetic Portuguese water dog. I threw a ball into the pond, and the pups competed in swimming out to get it. A powerhouse in the water, Finley often triumphed over Mountain Girl. Her parent, having an almost constant smile, told me that her dog was named after one of the members of Ken Kesey's gang called the Merry Pranksters. Ken Kesey was a pioneer in the psychedelic movement. High on LSD, the gang roamed the streets of San Francisco in the late '60s and early '70s, making faces at passersby and creating other public disturbances which caused the FBI to pursue them.

In an excerpt from the book *The Electric Kool-Aid Acid Test*, the fundamental book on hippies, written in 1968 by Tom Wolfe, "Mountain Girl is a tall girl, big and beautiful with dark brown hair falling down to her shoulders except that the lower two-thirds of her falling hair looks like a paintbrush dipped in cadmium yellow from where she dyed it blond in Mexico."

While the pups continued racing through the water, I continued to converse with Mountain Girl's mama. You're way too young to have been a hippie," I said.

She replied, "When I was sixteen and all the kids were moving to Haight-Ashbury (a neighborhood in San Francisco) for an acid-based life, my friends and I emulated them in every way. I loved Mountain Girl's personality and decided that someday I would have a dog named after her."

When we left Eagle Pond, Finley was not tired; he had plenty of oomph left for more activities. We had been invited to spend the afternoon at a friend's pool. Soon after we arrived, my friend Judy opened the pool gate. Finley ran to the pool and launched himself forward with a stretch that made him look like a Frisbee-seeking missile, body and limbs parallel to the water! He touched down, causing a big splash. We were all amazed, having never seen him do this before.

Finley continued to fly through the air with the greatest of ease...

Finley takes a flying leap into a pool.   **Finley is about to splash down.**

A Visit to Concord

August 26, 2021

🐾

Consider how remote and novel Gowing's Swamp is. Beneath it is a quaking bed of sphagnum and in it grow plants that scarcely a citizen of Concord ever sees. It would be as novel to them to stand there as in a conservatory or in Greenland.
—Henry David Thoreau, August 30, 1856

Thoreau referenced Gowing's Swamp in 37 entries in his Journal, in Walden and his essay "Walking." The bog was formed when plants that lived on the edges of the pond began moving out deeper into the water as the subarctic climate warmed. Their thick tangle of roots, along with sphagnum moss built up after many years.
—a trail signpost created by the Sudbury Valley Trustees

Finley and I hadn't anticipated the serenity that we would find by walking the 0.9-mile loop trail around Gowing's Swamp in Concord. Perhaps it was the sense of being in a rare landscape that looked like it did 350 years ago. Maybe the fact that we met just one lone hiker along the way who helped us experience the peacefulness of this beautiful Sunday morning?

We began our trek by walking through the Playscape at the Ripley School. Finley was elated, having never been to a playground before; carrying his ball, he jumped over the round wood sections that lay on the ground. Finally, he the area and followed me as I entered the oak and pine woods. After a few minutes, we crossed paths with a woman who, after briefly observing Finley, pronounced, "Have you talked with him about not going into the swamp?"

"Not yet," I replied, "but I will—good idea!" We smiled, having shared a sweet moment.

When Finley and I reached the edge of the bog which was tucked below a glacial ridge, I decided not to have that conversation with him. I reasoned that for Finley, the whole point of visiting a bog area necessitated that he be in the bog itself. Finley turned to me, waiting for my approval to explore it, and I gave him my okay. He dropped down into the mud at the edge of the bog. When he eventually came out, I saw that his bottom half was covered with a thick layer of mud. He looked like an impossible combination of a black Lab and a yellow Lab. Did I mention that his face was muddy as well?

What is the definition of a quaking bog? According to the National Geographic Society, "Quaking bogs develop over a lake or a pond with bog mats, thick layers of vegetation about a meter (3 feet) thick on top. Quaking bogs bounce when people or animals walk on them giving them their name."

Finley never reached the bog mats beyond the mud. Had he done so, I believe that he would have sunk into the floating sphagnum or peat moss mats.

Finley's cleanup was pretty miserable; he shook water-laced mud all over me. I washed and re washed him. Still the mud lingered.

You reap what you sow, I later thought. Maybe it's all worth it in the service of having another one of the pup's adventures.

Finley is playing in the thicket.

Finley Enjoys a Visit to Bearly Read Books

September 2, 2021

🐾

**You can't deny laughter; when it comes, it plops down
in your favorite chair and stays as long as it wants.
—Stephen King, author of at least 133 books**

Perhaps you think this is a little nuts, but occasionally I like to read illustrated children's books to Finley. It is another form of connection for us.

A couple of weeks ago I was visiting Bearly Read Books, a used bookstore in Sudbury, to pick up two books that I had ordered. I noticed a woman seated in an upholstered armchair, reading to a child. I queried Betty Ann Sharp, the proprietor, to find out if dogs were permitted into her shop.

"Well behaved dogs are always allowed here," she replied. "Only one dog at a time, and if a visitor is scared of dogs, the dogs may not come in." She spoke of a cockatoo and two hedgehogs having also come in for a visit.

A rottweiler came in last week and put his large head on her lap, while his parent spent time browsing in the stacks. She told me about kids and dogs showing up with an adult in tow, who then reads a story to them.

On a day when the shop was closed, Betty Ann unlocked the door and welcomed Finley and me in for a personal visit; Finley was allowed to enter unleashed since it didn't seem that he would get into any trouble.

I have always wondered why this used bookstore was named Bearly Read Books instead of Barely Read Books. Originally, books and stuffed animals were sold here by the store's first proprietor. The story goes that when he was a newlywed, his wife whimsically mentioned that he ought to open a bookstore since he had so many books!

Thirty-two years passed, and he was ready to sell his shop. Betty Ann Sharp, a high school English teacher, decided (also based on a whim) to buy it! Now she buys and sells rare and used books. She often hears her patrons exclaim in delight when they find a book that they haven't seen for many years; she takes great pleasure in hearing their joyous comments.

Finley plopped down by her side as she began one of the three stories that can be found in the book: *Three Stories That You Can Read to Your Dog* by Sara Swan Miller and illustrated by True Kelley. Finley looked up as she read the dramatic story and wagged his tail in approval.

It was now time for Finley to begin a self-guided tour of the passageways lined with books. He stopped to sniff an old edition of "Treasure Island." He stopped to kiss Betty Ann who was waiting for him to appear during his run-through.

When Finley finished his tour, he spotted a little teddy bear near the front window of the shop. Finley always loves new toys, even if they are acquired by ill-gotten means. He reached up to retrieve the teddy bear.

Who said, "It didn't seem that he would get into any trouble?"

Finley is visiting Bearly Read Books in Sudbury.

Affectionate Finley stops to kiss the proprietor, Betty Ann Sharp.

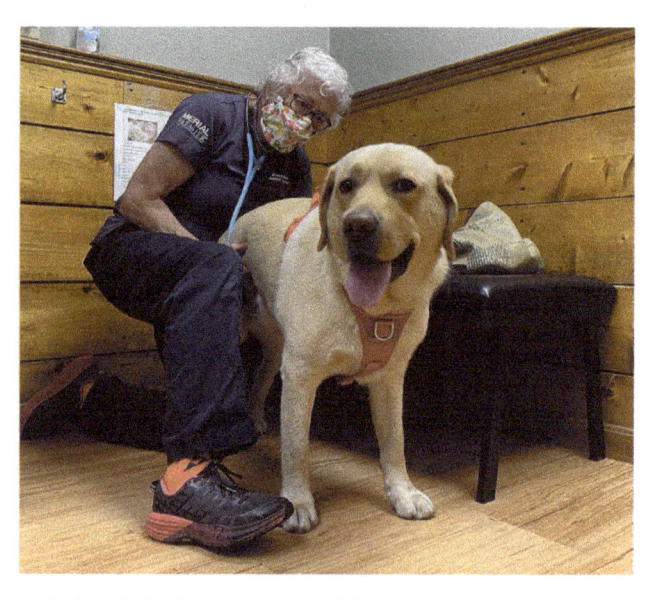

Finley is being examined by Dr. Susan Rabaut.

Finley Visits His Favorite Veterinarian

September 9, 2021

A Labrador retriever speaks: "Hey there! Can I lick your ice cream cone? Can we see your friends with the kids who drop food? Oh wait, can we see my buds at the dog park? Never mind, I think I want to play fetch, collapse and then snuggle. I know that it seems like I'm the extrovert in overdrive, but at the end of the day, I'm one of the most loyal dogs, and smartest too, on the planet. I have so many things I like to do. And if we're honest, I probably have more friends than you. Just kidding! Ultimately, I always choose you."

—20 Most Loyal Breeds That Will Always Be By Your Side, *Reader's Digest*

During the last couple of months, I was surprised to hear Finley making strange rasping sounds within a few minutes of starting his outdoor play. I chalked it up to these greater than normal hot, humid days. One morning, when Finley was playing soccer with his big red ball, I began to wonder if he had a small blockage in his esophagus, causing the rasping sounds. I made an appointment with his veterinarian post haste. Dr. Susan Rabaut, who practices at the Framingham Animal Hospital, has been a vet for fifty-three years and is regarded as a top diagnostician and surgeon; she has successfully treated all my dogs for the past thirty-five years.

Some dogs are fearful of going to the vet; when they enter the facility, they sniff the environment, which can trigger unhappy memories of being examined by a relatively unknown person. Dr. Rabaut explained that during the last eighteen months of the COVID-19 environment where dogs have limited exposure to new experiences, they are more hesitant and anxious when they come into the hospital.

Finley, on the other hand, loves to visit with his vet, the nurses, the vet techs, the secretaries and others, though he is kind enough to stay away from very sick animals.

At the appointed time, Finley bounded through the hospital door, restrained by a short, thick leash. He was directed to the weighing station. Dr. Rabaut, who describes Finley as "an open, accepting happy dog with a great personality," began to examine him while he intermittently wagged his tail. "There is nothing wrong with Finley except that he has gained ten pounds in twelve months and that is the cause of the problem," she declared.

His tapered waist had disappeared! How could I not have noticed?

Dr. Rabaut added, "With a reduction of his chow from four to three cups a day, he should lose ten pounds in two to three months." Additionally, I was told to add more green beans to his diet. The added fiber would make him feel fuller, as if a Lab could ever feel full.

Finley wagged his enthusiastic goodbyes to the secretarial staff as we were paying our bill. I suspect that he would have loved to plant goodbye kisses on them as well.

"Finley, perhaps putting you on a diet will be easier than putting myself on a diet," I said. "In no time I'll be taking pictures of your beautiful new svelte self!"

Finley Swims and Retrieves under a Waterfall

September 16, 2021

🐾

Dogs can swim 1-2 mph depending on the type of breed, some breeds will swim slower than this, if at all. Dogs with webbed feet such as the Portuguese water spaniel will be able to swim the fastest.
—Pathway Pooch, "How Fast Can Dogs Swim?"

From September 1 through 3, five and a half more inches of rain fell, making the grass happy and thrilling Finley, but many of my annual flowers drowned.

On the morning of September 4, instead of departing for unexplored landscapes, I unexpectedly stopped in the middle of our driveway with another thought in mind. I asked Finley if he wanted to go back to the waterfall under the big bridge spanning Hop Brook. Since Finley is a most agreeable pup, it was a foregone conclusion that he would indicate a yes. It never hurts to ask.

Finley has had many adventures there, the most memorable being the time when he served as the companion and helper to a beaver specialist who, with his clam rake, was dislodging sticks from the top of the falls, which were partially blocking the brook from flowing downstream.

The water was moving fast; undeterred, Finley jumped in. He had the good sense not to swim too close to the center of the brook where the current ran fastest. Had he ignored his perception, he would have been swept away, though unhurt by the flat, obstacle-free current. Finley would have been surprised by the free ride but would have easily gone with the flow. A good lesson.

While Finley was enjoying the water, I walked down to a spot where the falls tumbled over the rock bed. I found a seat on a smooth rock and got lost in the sounds of the crashing water. Moving water produces negatively-charged ions that increase levels of the mood chemical serotonin, helping to alleviate depression, relieve stress and boost our day time energy.

I couldn't possibly hear the approach of a woman and her handsome and muscular black Lab puppy as they came down the little hill very close to my rock. Thunder, the nine-month-old puppy, was straining at his short leash, his eyes following Finley who was still swimming. Thunder's soft whimpers soon became full-blown cries.

As if she were reading my mind, the woman declared, "Once he hits the water, he never swims back. My last Lab was afraid of the water, and now Thunder won't leave it!"

"Would he stick with Finley?" I asked.

"Maybe, but I don't know for sure," she replied.

I began to imagine Thunder swimming and floating downstream through the three rivers that discharge into the Gulf of Maine in Newburyport. The lower twenty-two miles of the third river, the Merrimack River, are tidal. So if the tide were coming in, Thunder would not have been able to power through it and reach the ocean. My reverie had a happy ending, though. The pup reached the ocean and was met with a round of applause.

So far, Finley has peacefully canoed on sections of the Sudbury and Concord rivers. Maybe someday we'll rent a sea kayak and float down the last twenty-two miles of the Merrimack River on an outgoing tide?

Finley is trying to locate a stick that is underwater.

Chillaxing

September 23, 2021

Finley and I have gone to the beach for the week and are having a wonderful time together, as always. In lieu of this week's adventure, I am submitting two poems written by Mary Oliver from her wonderful book of poetry entitled *Dog Songs*.

How It Begins

A puppy is a puppy is a puppy.
He's probably in a basket with a bunch
of other puppies.
Then he's a little older and he's nothing
but a bundle of longing.
He doesn't even understand it.
Then someone picks him up and
says, "I want this one."

The Sweetness of Dogs

What do you say, Percy? I am thinking
of sitting out on the sand to watch
the moon rise. It's full tonight.
So we go.
And the moon rises, so beautiful it
makes me shudder, makes me think
about time and space, makes me take
measure of myself: one iota
pondering heaven. Thus we sit, myself
thinking how grateful I am for the
moon's perfect beauty and also, oh! how rich
it is to love the world. Percy, meanwhile,
leans against me and gazes up into
my face. As though I were just as
wonderful as the perfect moon.

Finley relaxing

A tired pup

Finley is retrieving a tennis ball in Cape Cod Bay.

Finley Spends Four days in Old Cape Cod, Part 1: Cape Cod Bay

September 30, 2021

🐾

If you're fond of sand dunes and salty air
Quaint little villages here and there
You're sure to fall in love with Old Cape Cod
—C. Rothrock/M. Yakus/I. Pinkus, "Old Cape Cod"

(The single was recorded by Patti Page and became a gold record, having sold more than a million copies.)

I heard Cape Cod's unofficial anthem in 1957, soon after it was released. As a dreamy nine-year-old, I was captured by the song's sentimental images of a seemingly faraway place.

"Where is Old Cape Cod?" I remember asking my mom this question as we stood in the pink bedroom that I shared with my younger sister in Brooklyn, New York. She didn't know. Nine years passed before I first made my way across the Sagamore Bridge, spanning the Cape Cod Canal which separates the Cape from mainland Massachusetts.

Finley, being a youngster, had not as yet dug down (literally) into the pleasures of the cape. "You know, Finley, September is my favorite month to be on the cape. Let's go down for a few days; the crowds are gone, and the bay and ocean waters are nice and warm." I added, "Besides, I'll share a lobster roll with you!"

Finley knew that I was onto something good. We checked into a pet-friendly hotel on the bay side of a town on the lower cape, staying in the room just long enough to open the windows. Ah, Cape Cod Bay was before us. In keeping with Finley's extreme eagerness and enthusiasm, he made a mad dash for the water. I reached for one of his well-worn tennis balls, and the swimming and retrieving game began. The high-tide reached right up to the lounge chairs located next to the back stairs of the hotel. This was not a storm surge from a coastal storm, nor was the full moon expected for another week.

Between tennis ball launches, I noticed a woman walking along the beach, who with eyes half closed and wearing large pink earphones that dwarfed her ears, was swaying gracefully, moving her arms up and down by her sides. She was enveloped in a cloud of marijuana smoke. I turned toward Finley and saw that his nose was wriggling; otherwise, he didn't seem to take note of the woman's happy walk along the beach.

It was now 6:00 p.m., and the golden light of late afternoon was upon us. Finley and I were on our way back to the motel when we stopped to look at a simply gorgeous garden that fronted an old cape house.

The owner called out to us from behind his screened window, "Beautiful dog you have there." I was hoping to take a photo of an unleashed Finley in the owner's beautifully-lit garden, but I hesitated at first.

"Yes," was his answer, "I'll be right out." After taking a couple of shots of my big yellow dog, I fell into an easy conversation with Bruce, the owner. We didn't notice Finley until we heard the splash; Finley had jumped into Bruce's lily pond which was a few feet away! In an instant Bruce reached the pond and yanked a surprised Finley out. My apology was met with laughter.

"Don't worry, dogs do this all the time," Bruce said. "Besides, the lily pads will repair themselves by tomorrow."

Finley is being yanked out of a lily pond.

At left, Finley is sitting by a handmade sign on Race Point Beach.

Above, Finley has a blast in the ocean.

Old Cape Cod, Part 2: Two Ocean Beaches

October 7, 2021

🐾

Sunshine, blue eyes, tan lines, slow tide
—Jake Owen, "Beachin"

The coastal waters of Cape Cod are influenced by two sharply different ocean currents. The Labrador current flows down the northeast coast bringing cold arctic waters to the beaches of Maine and Massachusetts. Concurrently, the warmer Gulf Stream travels up from the south and swings east to cross the Atlantic Ocean in the vicinity of Nantucket.

Beaches on the Atlantic Ocean side of the forty-mile stretch of the National Seashore from Eastham to Provincetown, including Chatham to the south, are considered the coldest. The protected waters of Cape Cod Bay are mostly warmer, though there are a few warm pockets on the ocean side.

It was now day two of our four-day Cape Cod adventure. Finley and I planned to spend the day at Head of the Meadow beach, an ocean-side beach in North Truro. Truro had once been called Dangerfield for its treacherous coastline. The pup and I walked the pathway up the leeward side of the dune. Since Finley has not as yet acquired his own dog packs, I was the pack animal, schlepping two extra-large beach bags filled to the brim with everything needed to spend a proper day on the beach. When we reached the dune's apex the sparking ocean and broad sandy beach opened before us. Dangerfield?

Not today. A temperature of seventy-five degrees with a clear blue sky were our offerings. The beach was empty save for a lone dot of a person walking along the beach in the direction of Provincetown. The tide was out and Finley headed toward the ocean. Naturally. It was mid-September and for a New Englander the water was warm, in fact warm enough for me to run right in without needing to desensitize to colder water found in the earlier summer months.

Did my friend Judy first spot the fin of a Great White Shark swimming close to shore? I think so. Finley and I left the water and walked parallel to the shore focusing on the shark's fin. We saw the sweet face of a seal who with her head above water, was looking at us. We locked gazes and I silently prayed that she would live to a ripe old age.

The waters of Cape Cod have one of the largest concentrations of great white sharks in the world. They patrol along the coast, drawn into the shallow water to feed on the grey seals. The scary part is that they spend an average of 45 percent of their time in water less than fifteen-feet deep. As one result, surfing is becoming a thing of the past on the cape.

The shark was now out-of-sight and Finley and I cautiously returned to the water for more play. Time passed and Finley's second favorite activity of the day began, that is, running over my blue and yellow blanket and shaking his wet coat all over me. This was not a real problem, although I screeched every time he did it. When he began to dig in the sand and fling it backward onto the blanket and me, I had enough! I called him off though I softened when I saw the artistic, abstract sand patterns that he created on our blanket.

We spent our third day at Race Point Beach in Provincetown. Finley met a handful of dogs, but could not entice any of them to join him in the water.

Day three was pretty much a copy of day two, minus the sharks.

For that, I am glad.

Old Cape Cod, Part 3: The Dunes and the Lighthouse

October 14, 2021

🐾

A steady wind sweeping across the beach carries grains of sand inland. When its motion is interrupted by a log or grass clump, the wind drops its burden of sand. Slowly a mound builds up. Growing higher, broader, merging with other mounds, it becomes a hillock, a ridge, a dune. If nothing anchors the sand, the dune will creep inland.
—Dorothy Sterling, *The Outer Lands*

On September 10, a Cape Air flight departing from Boston skidded off the runway in Provincetown and crash landed into the nearby woods. All seven people aboard the plane were seriously hurt. The next day, my friends were traveling along a road adjacent to the crash site in order to reach the office that issues sand permits for all terrain vehicles. By obtaining the permit, we would be free to ride through the P-town dunes. My friends were turned back because the road was closed for two days due to the plane crash.

Today was day four of Finley's Cape Cod adventures. The road was now open, the permit granted and we piled into the Jeep, bracing ourselves for the bumpy ride ahead. We stopped to air down (deflate the tire pressure), a necessity to effectively traverse the dunes.

The Jeep began to rock from side to side and roll from front to back. Finley became alarmed; he drew closer to me and began to yelp. I scooped him up into my arms and held him, applying a firm, though gentle, constant pressure in order to calm him down. I became his thunder vest. It helped. We rounded Race Point Lighthouse and reached the far side of Race Point Beach.

Finley didn't need or want to rest even after three days of intense play: swimming, running, retrieving, and digging. I wanted to rest, so I decided to lie down on the wet sand and feel the tide come in around me. With a small underwater camera attached to my wrist, I looked up from my low vantage point to see Finley digging in the nearby sand. The photo practically took itself.

Built in 1797, Highland Light in North Truro is one of the oldest lighthouses in the country.

Ocean waves continually hammer at the cliffs, causing erosion. In the early 1990s the lighthouse looked perilously close to the ocean. In 1996, the light was moved 450 feet back from its original site.

Finley, his friend Gizmo and the humans were on our way to visit this quintessential New England lighthouse. Since I had visited it before its move, I began to tell Finley what he could expect to see. We walked the narrow pathway that led to the lighthouse. What we saw instead was a tower covered in scaffolding; we didn't know that Highland Light was undergoing major repairs. If Finley was disappointed by this turn of events, he didn't show it.

Oh yes, as I promised Finley on day one, we shared a lobster roll. It was a terrific one filled to the brim with warm chunks of fresh lobster meat. I gave him a large chunk and then another for good measure.

Finley, my friends and I had had an outstanding four days together on Old Cape Cod.

Finley is digging in the sand to his heart's content.

Finley is waiting to alight from the Jeep.

Making Friends with Courtney

October 21, 2021

🐾

    Finley is a friendly, attentive and loving listener, the likes of which I have never seen before in a dog. Amazement and appreciation for his being a great partner in our daily walks. I love Finley. When he is let out the front door he waits until I'm out before running down the small hill to the backyard. Frequently, he turns back and slows down to ensure that I catch up to him, which takes me longer these days. When I call out, "Finley," he stops his carousing, looks up and heeds what I tell him. It never ceases to amaze me how responsive and cooperative he is. He deserves superstar status.
    —Linda Fields, his loving aunt from New York City

Finley has another devoted fan, one formerly unknown to us.

On September 12, we received a letter written by Eunice Whipple, a longtime Sudbury resident. The focus of her letter was her third child, forty-six-year-old Courtney, who was born with the genetic disease tuberous sclerosis.

Courtney adores dogs. Soon after Finley's Adventures began to appear in the Crier, Eunice told me that she showed the weekly stories to her daughter.

"Courtney's reaction was one of complete joy." Together, they would laugh at his escapades. Eunice continued, "Then Courtney started looking for the next week's paper every Thursday."

Prior to the publication of Finley's column, Courtney had never enjoyed reading.

"Then we started cutting out the weekly articles and leaving them on the coffee table so that we could see Finley's pictures all week."

Eunice politely asked how I would feel about bringing Finley over for a short, surprise field trip to their home.

Perhaps Courtney could throw a tennis ball out for Finley to retrieve?

When I told Finley about our invitation, I didn't get past "tennis ball" before he looked up and showed his enthusiasm for yet another adventure.

Finley jumped out of the car and saw Courtney walking down the stairs that led to her front lawn. He sped toward her, so happy to meet her, that he jumped up intending to give her a kiss. Within minutes Courtney began to toss one of Finley's tennis balls to her favorite pup.

Later, when Finley sat by Courtney's side, Courtney showed me a handsome scrapbook that she and her mom had created; every page displayed one of Finley's past adventures.

Courtney related that she was first attracted to his photos and then to all the fun he was having. She felt that she was part of his life.

I asked Courtney if she might like to take a short walk with Finley to a small bridge in town from which she could toss sticks or a ball and watch Finley swim off to get them.

We would dress ourselves in red, orange or yellow and look like giant autumn leaves. Courtney said yes, and we arranged a future date.

Eunice and I spoke a few days later. "After meeting Finley, Courtney comes out of her room with a smile on her face," Eunice said. "Thinking of Finley?"

"Yes," Courtney replied.

When Finley and I were saying our goodbyes after a wonderful ninety-minute visit, Courtney quietly said to me, "You made my dream come true."

PS. This wonderful encounter made me think of the line from the song "Nature Boy" by Nat King Cole: "The greatest thing you'll ever learn is just to love and be loved in return."

Finley and Courtney enjoy playing ball together.

Courtney proudly displays her Finley scrapbook.

Visiting Newburyport's Waterfront

October 28, 2021

🐾

    The life-affirming zest that flavors moments big and. small has a language all its own. Adventure is life lived at high pitch, even when the adventures are small in cosmic scope. A trip to the beach may become an adventure, unleashing a surprising gust of joy.
    —"What Adventures Know Could Fill a Book,"
Boston Globe

Finley and I were on our way to Newburyport Harbor on a warm and sunny late September day.

We had booked a tour with Yankee Clipper Harbor Tours for an excursion that would take us down the last few miles of the Merrimack River and deposit us into the ocean on the far side of Newburyport.

Finley and I were the first passengers to walk down the gangplank into the forty-two-passenger boat.

Finley hesitated, unsure of himself at first, but when he received a big welcome from the waiting captain, he scampered down the walkway, his fear vanishing.

Surprisingly few passengers came aboard that day; some of them stopped to pet Finley, receiving heavy-duty tail wags in return.

Finley sat next to me on a wide bench in the middle of the boat. He reveled in the smell of the salt air and took in the many sights along the way.

On the starboard side of the boat we passed nine-mile-long Plum Island which loses an appalling six inches to one foot of sand every year due to the inexorable rising tides.

We saw dozens of people in the water and on the beach. On the port side we saw the Isle of Shoals in New Hampshire, known for its excellent fishing, whale watching and recorded shipwrecks.

We looked north across the Gulf of Maine to see York, Maine, punctuated by 692-feet high Mount Agamenticus.

Finally, the river emptied into the Atlantic Ocean and we reversed course. Finley jumped off the bench and sat down on the boat's floor.

He never saw the two squirrels swimming across the Merrimack, which here at its widest, was two miles crossways.

We had lunch on the patio of a nearby dog-friendly restaurant. Along the side of each perimeter table sat a young puppy.

Finley was pleased to meet a ten-week-old Airedale, also named Finley. He greeted a four-month-old black Labrador puppy and a six-month-old golden retriever puppy.

The human baby sitting in a high chair was completely ignored by all, save her family.

Finley is seated in the captain's chair.

Newburyport, birthplace of the Coast Guard, has an attractive waterfront with winding walkways along the Merrimack River.

After lunch, Finley and I said our goodbyes to the puppies and began our stroll. He was drawn to a particular golden retriever named Sully who was named after Captain "Sully" Sullenberger, the hero, who on January 15, 2009, was piloting the plane that shortly after taking off from LaGuardia Airport in Queens, struck a flock of birds and lost all engine power.

Sully glided the plane onto the Hudson River, saving all 155 passengers aboard who were rescued by nearby boats.

While Finley and Sully were inhaling each other's smells, I told Sully's mom that we had never been to Newburyport's waterfront before and that Finley and I were having a grand time. She promptly invited us to join them for a twenty-minute walk along the shore to Joppa Flats, a stretch of the river where clam shacks proliferated in the late nineteenth century.

A boat ramp crossing the flats gave Finley and Sully access to the water. Since there weren't any sticks or balls around to toss, I picked up a large handful of wet seaweed and threw it out into the water. With two well-matched retrievers, the race was on.

That was exactly how we spent the rest of the afternoon, the humans laughing, taking turns propelling the seaweed through the air, while the pups excitedly playing their newfound game, Race to the Seaweed.

Finley and I didn't want the day to end.

Finley and Sully are waiting for the seaweed toss.

154

Sunrise atop Mount Greylock

Finley is running toward the Veterans War Memorial Tower

A Surprise for Finley

November 4, 2021

The wonder of the world, the beauty and the power, the shapes of things, their colours, lights and shades; these I saw. Look ye also while life lasts.

—B.B.

I had a surprise for Finley which I didn't disclose until we were well underway. We were headed out to western Massachusetts to spend a few days at Bascom Lodge on top of Mount Greylock, the highest mountain in the state. Leaf-peeping and hiking with hopes of sharing a beautiful sunrise with Fin were in the basic plans as we embarked on this clear Tuesday morning in early October.

With an elevation of 3,489 feet, the summit of Mount Greylock features the only subalpine environment in Massachusetts. The mountain dominates the landscape. "To behold the mountain and witness its excellent majesty," as Herman Melville perceived it, calls for spending the night.

In two and a half hours, Finley and I reached the base of the mountain, ascending about eight miles of uninterrupted S curves. Finley sniffed the heavenly scent of freshly fallen wet leaves. He sensed that the end of our journey was nigh; he was raring to get out and go. Had he not worn a seat belt, I believe that he would have leaped clear out of the open window!

Bascom Lodge is a rustic arts and crafts lodge built in the late 1930s and constructed of local stone and old-growth, hand-hewn red spruce timbers blending beautifully into the landscape. Some of the through-hikers on the nearby Appalachian Trail treat themselves to a night at the lodge.

Just as Finley and I were checking in, his dear friend Bo suddenly appeared at the lodge's entryway. Both pups strained at the leash to greet one another. We were on the trail soon after that grand entrance. The relatively short loop trail began at a kiosk behind the lodge and descended rapidly until we reached a hard-to-negotiate series of large jagged rocks and slippery boulders. The hiking poles which would have provided balance were left back at the lodge! Meanwhile, Finley and Bo were running down the trail and back up again not bothered by the difficult terrain. We turned back.

The next morning, Finley, Bo, Pippa, and I stood on the eastern summit to await sunrise. We were alone. Fog blanketed the Hoosic River Valley and the town of Adams below us. When the first point of light appeared above the clouds, Finley came over and sat quietly by my side. We stayed to watch the yellow striated light broaden. We breathed in that exquisite view.

Dedicated in 1933, the ninety-two-foot-high Veterans War Memorial Tower on top of Greylock is Massachusetts' official commemoration of its war dead. It is made from slabs of Quincy granite and is topped with a globe-shaped beacon. Finley and Bo resumed scouting and playing in an area close to the tower.

Now, it was time for breakfast.

Errands around Town

November 11, 2021

🐾

The development of food freezing techniques was one of the more important food adventures in culinary history. We all have Clarence Frank Birdseye II to thank for this. Birdseye's claim to fame was the quick-freezing method that he introduced in 1924. He saw natives catching fish in 50 below zero weather, which froze stiff as soon as they were taken out of the water. The Inuit also showed Birdseye how to preserve fresh vegetables in tubs and buckets of water in the cold weather, freezing the vegetables for later use.

—thymemachinecuisine.com

At 8:30 a.m., October 20, Finley and I were playing a vigorous game of ChuckIt in the expanse of our backyard. The twenty-six-inch-long arm of the plastic toy ends in a notched semicircle perfect for holding and then launching a tennis ball. The long arc of the ChuckIt permitted me to hurl the ball from left field to home plate, bypassing second base, had we been playing ball at Fenway Park. More than a slight exaggeration. In any case, Finley ran at top speed to reach the ball and stayed at it for about fifteen minutes.

Finally, he sat down in a shady section of the grass and with all senses alive, took pleasure in having a short break.

Not much time passed before I was ready to go out and do a couple of errands. Though my departure was taking place during Finley's nap time, he woke up, ran to the door, looked up into my face and then over to the door. And then again. "C'mon, boy, let's go," was all I could say.

Our first stop was at Sudbury Automotive for a gas fill up. Tim and Aron, fast and efficient attendants, came over to say hi when they saw Finley. With eyes closed, Finley delighted in receiving lots of concurrent petting from his two new friends. I consider myself a patron of this gas station for two reasons. I love to see what vintage tees Tim is wearing the day that I roll up to the gas pump. I have seen him in He Man, Ninja Turtles and Transformer tees which are some of his favorite childhood characters. The second reason that I like to go to this station is that the gas prices are good. I asked the guys if they kept a stash of dog biscuits for their four-legged customers. "Usually yes, but we're out of them," was the reply. Since Finley had had a full breakfast topped with blueberries and later a salmon nugget after his morning exertions, I was sure that he didn't mind the lack of another treat, though Labrador Retrievers have a genetic peculiarity which makes them feel hungry all the time.

The next stop was at the Farmer's Market in Wayland. Lots of people and a couple of other pups were shopping there on this, the last day of the summer market. Finley and I ventured over to see Clark, whose Lazio Family Farm is located in Ashby near the New Hampshire border. Clark recognized Finley from a previous Finley adventure last October and gave him a hearty hello and a homemade rawhide chew. Notice Finley (in the photo) receiving his present. He devoured it in no time.

Finley and I stood in line at one of the fruit and vegetable stands. I surveyed the tables that held large heads of white cauliflower, purple Japanese eggplants and red crunchy McGowan apples. I recalled the times back in the 1950s when we city folk ate flash-frozen vegetables that were infinitely superior to the awful canned peas and carrots that I eventually refused to eat. Though many of the frozen vegetables are okay, they don't compare to the locally-sourced produce that was spread out before me.

The winter market is scheduled to open on January 8. Planned are twenty-five indoor stands and twenty-five outdoor stands. Even if the outdoor thermometer records a temperature of twenty degrees, Finley will be ready to visit the outdoor stands.

After all, a treat is sure to be in the offing for our dear Finley.

Tim and Aron are enjoying petting Finley.

Clark has given Finley a rawhide chew.

A Trip to Forty Caves

November 18, 2021

🐾

At Forty Caves, glacial erratics, large rocks and boulders moved by advancing ice sheets, are evidence of the last ice age. Most of these rocks are granite with feldspar crystals and match those in Northern Massachusetts. It is these erratics that have slipped and slid together which form the caves. Local legend holds that the smooth, round depressions in the rock at Forty Caves once held quartz that Native Americans once used for spear points. They popped the quartz nodules out of the surrounding rock with a combination of heat and cold.

—James William Skehan, *Roadside Geology of Massachusetts*

Try as we might, Finley and I could not find the actual caves located within the Forty Caves conservation area. We departed on our hike from the Francis Street entrance in Clinton, thinking that we would reach the caves within thirty minutes.

Though the cave site wasn't shown on the map, I had been informed that a tiny trail that left the main trail between the B and C markers on the blue trail would eventually lead us to the caves. We never found that tiny trail.

Instead, Finley and I cut through the wooded terrain in the direction of the X that I inked on the map to indicate our destination.

"Finley, go find the caves," I said, but for once, Finley had no idea what I was talking about.

With increasing frustration, I renamed our destination the Lost Caves. We found our way back to the main trail.

The Clinton-Newbury fault system is visible in several spots at Forty Caves. Rocks split under the pressure of fault movement.

As we continued with our hike, we viewed a landscape replete with spectacular geologic formations.

There were steep bedrock cliffs and glacial erratics that measured up to thirty feet in diameter.

Finley and I walked alongside gurgling North Brook, a tributary of the Assabet River. The brook invited us to sit for a while and listen to its sweet sounds.

We sat by a photogenic rock overhang through which the brook made its way downstream. We shared a crisp Macon apple, one of many that I had bought at a local apple orchard.

It was clear to me that after two failed attempts to reach the caves, Finley and I needed a guide. Dan Stimson, the Sudbury Valley Trustees' Director of Stewardship, agreed to guide us. He suggested that we depart from the Allen Road entrance in Berlin. We walked through a jigsaw puzzle of Berlin, Clinton and SVT land. We followed the winding trail downhill and crossed one of SVT's recently constructed wooden bridges. Hikers no longer need to traverse the stream by walking/hopping from rock to rock.

We reached our destination. A broad line of 30-foot-high caves stood before us: a perfect habitat for mountain lions, coyotes and black bears! Finley dipped down into the brook and then proceeded to make his way up the ancient tumbled rock wall. He turned to sniff at the entrance to one of the caves.

"Come down," I sharply called out. He obliged, good puppy that he is.

I hugged Finley right before he jumped into the backseat of our car.

"We did it, Finley, but not without the help from Dan, our knowledgeable guide."

Finley is retrieving a stick from North Brook.

Finley is surrounded by boulders at Forty Caves.

Photogenic Finley Wishes You a Happy Thanksgiving

November 25, 2021

🐾

Finley is watching a glorious sunrise

Joy comes from simple and natural things, mists over meadows, sunlight on leaves, the path of the moon over water. Even rain and wind and stormy clouds bring joy, just as knowing animals and flowers and where they live.

—Sigurd F. Olson

Instead of recounting one of Finley's newest adventures today, I want to show you some previously unpublished photos of the big yellow pup.

As you can easily see, Finley plays with gusto, watches carefully at everything going on around him, and takes the time to appreciate the power and beauty of a stunning sunrise.

Finley and I want to wish you a joyous and healthy Thanksgiving. Additionally, we would like to quote a small section of an earth prayer, written by the Rabbi Rami M. Shapiro:

My friends, let us give thanks for Wonder.
Let us give thanks for the Wonder of Life
that infuses all things now and forever.
Each of us is unique
coming into the world with a gift no other can offer
We eat to nourish the vehicle of giving,
We eat to sustain our task of world repair,
our quest for harmony, peace and justice.

Finley visits the old pet cemetery in Greenways.

Stirring Up Friendly Spirits along the Sudbury River

December 2, 2021

> Greenways Conservation Area is a portion of the former Paine Estate, purchased in 1995 by Sudbury Valley Trustees and the town of Wayland. With Heard Farm Conservation Area across the river and Great Meadows Wildlife Refuge extending both up and downstream, this stretch of the river, along with Heard Pond, is renowned for its biological richness.
> —SVT brochure describing the property

At mile marker 18.9 on the Sudbury River (river's length measures 31.2 miles), one can find a canoe landing and a teeny foot trail leading up from the river, providing access to Greenways. Many years ago, I participated in a kayak/canoe tour that first led me to Greenways. I was entranced by the beauty and diversity of the property: old cart paths, mature evergreen and deciduous trees, historical sights, stunning river vistas, and one particular eccentricity.

Finley and I had last visited here in June during one of the heatwaves; since Finley cannot abide the heat, he spent part of that day partially submerged in the Sudbury River. I had intended to pen that adventure, but it got misplaced in the paper shuffle of Finley's many adventures.

A couple of afternoons ago we returned, accompanied by my friend Jeannie who had not as yet visited this charming landscape. We began our walk on one of the old cart paths edged by trees displaying the sun-splashed yellow foliage of a mid-November afternoon. Interspersed were evergreen trees providing a nice contrast to the scene before us. Finley sped ahead. Eventually, we turned right onto that teeny path that led us down to the river. It is said that today's paddlers and onlookers virtually see the same view that Native Americans saw as they traveled the river. It was quiet, dreamy musing. Finley swam and fetched to his heart's delight.

Afterward, Finley reached the animal cemetery and ran through it, perhaps stirring some friendly spirits who smiled when they saw him having such a grand time.

The cemetery was created by Virginia Lowe Paine as a final resting place for her pets. The cemetery and much of the surrounding conservation area were part of the former Paine Estate. The epitaphs are unique. Little Simmy was an orphaned monkey that Mrs. Paine found on safari in Africa. Simmy's epitaph reads: "This little life is woven with the substance of our home –1926-1960." Mrs. Paine stipulated that within any future purchase and sale's agreement of the property the pet cemetery had to be preserved and an easement provided for her family and friends.

Across from the animal cemetery and down a bit lies almost half a mile of the river's shoreline. The water sparkled.

To find beauty and holiness in so many ways. We did, that afternoon.

Looking back

Skills with a Softball

December 9, 2021

🐾

It is generally believed that softball developed from a game called indoor baseball, first played in Chicago in 1887. It became known in the U.S. by various names such as kitten ball, mush ball and diamond ball. The name "softball" was given to the game in 1926 because the ball used to be soft; however, in modern-day usage, the balls are hard.
—"Softball, " definition, rules, history and facts
Britannica

Finley is not a working dog, although others of his breed shine in doing police work, search and rescue, therapy and service work. I believe that Finley could excel in all of these areas with the possible exception of participating in therapy work. For example, should a client/patient begin to weep, Finley would come right over and kiss/lick their tears away. I know this to be true. The object of his affection might revel in receiving such a burst of compassion or laugh straight away. Actually, either of these results could be beneficial to the therapeutic process.

When Finley is not resting or sleeping, you can find him playing by himself or with others. My sister and brother were in town recently for a rare siblings' weekend; they love Finley and were looking forward to joining him for some outdoor fun. A couple of days before Linda and Howard flew up from warmer climes, I found the handle of my vintage wooden Louisville Slugger bat sticking out from under my bed. I placed it there as a means of protection prior to the installation of a real security system. Finley's ferocious barking at the sound of an intruder in the night would always be my first line of defense, though I've considered that given a liver or salmon treat by the villain, Finley would be mollified.

In any case, Finley jumped up to take my slugger away when we left the house the morning after my sibs arrived. I moved the bat way up over my head to keep it away from him because in Finley's mind bat equals a stick. Giving up, Finley soon found his red rubber football and began running with it in wide happy circles. I suddenly had an idea. Instead of having a session of softball batting and fielding practice, why don't we pair the bat and football and see where that takes us?

My brother swung hard, sometimes connecting with the wobbly football; on one occasion, Finley caught a high fly way out in left field. We roared with excitement.

When Finley first taught himself to play soccer, he used his nose and front legs to move the ball forward. The soccer ball rolled out to the base of a large tree in the woods and came to a halt. He looked confused, having no notion on how to proceed. I picked up his large red plastic soccer ball and tossed it back to the grass, whereupon he dribbled the ball about forty yards to the other end of the lawn. He ran the ball right or left, depending on what obstacles lay in his path. He was doing a fine job of practicing his agility drills. Now over a year has passed, and my sister and brother were amazed when Finley showed them his finely honed skills. What a day it was.

This morning I saw a video of a dog jumping on a trampoline that was surrounded by a safety enclosure. She was having the time of her life. This kind of exercise would not work for Finley. He cannot be so contained. After all, he played softball, football and soccer all in the course of an unbounded day!

Finley playing softball.

Finley is posing in front of the Babson Farm Quarry.

Finley is on top of a granite boulder at Halibut Point.

Finley Visits Halibut Point State Park

December 23, 2021

🐾

On the Cape Ann coastline, more reminiscent of Maine than Massachusetts, Halibut State Park and Halibut Reserve combine for a unique area of open space on this rocky headland. Originally called 'haul about' by sailors (because they had to tack around this mass of rock) Halibut Point was the site of numerous quarry operations which began in 1840, when the 450-million-year-old granite was cut, till 1929.
—Michael J. Tougias, *Nature Walks in Eastern Massachusetts*

The weather forecast for December 12 called for a clear windy day. By 9:30 a.m., the temperature had reached forty-six degrees. Finley and I were outside playing ball when a panoramic picture of the headlands at Halibut Point came to mind. Wouldn't it be great for Finley to smell the invigorating, salty air of Cape Ann, I mused? It wasn't necessary to ask Finley this time. By 10:00 a.m. we were on the road heading north.

Cape Ann is Massachusetts' other cape, though not as well-known as Cape Cod. Between Cape Cod and Cape Elizabeth, Maine, Cape Ann is the largest outcrop of rocky headland; the granite boulders, slab-like in many places and resistant to erosion, are a testament to the ice sheet that moved through the land fifteen thousand years ago.

We parked in a mostly empty lot and began to walk along a wide flat trail toward the open Atlantic. After five minutes, we reached the Babson Farm Quarry, a former source of granite for bridges, tunnels, monuments and buildings such as Boston's Custom House Tower. The quarry is filled to a depth of sixty feet with water derived from natural underground springs. The steep quarry walls rise far above the water. Many drownings have occurred here because people chose to jump in and weren't able to climb out.

Finley, being somewhat mature, knew enough not to get too close to the edge. Instead, he posed for a photo in front of the quarry, his right ear flapping in the wind.

Soon, the path opened to sweeping ocean views. We were standing on the northern tip of Cape Ann! With the help of a hiking stick, I picked my way down along the rocks. I turned around to see Finley standing on top of a large boulder; he was unsure how to proceed. He started to whimper. No matter how many times I tried to encourage him to move on, he wouldn't budge. I climbed back up on the boulder and showed him another but more circuitous way down. His left rear foot skidded on some wet seaweed just before he entered a large pool of ocean water, his sights set on one of his new tennis balls. Within minutes, quick-study Finley had mastered the difference between running on dry seaweed and skirting the slippery tangles of the wet kind.

After a while, I perched on a boulder and looked out to see the coastline of New Hampshire and southern Maine. Eventually, Finley joined me, his body stretched out by my side. We saw, heard and smelled the incoming tide hitting the rocks with greater and greater intensity. We sat there for a long time.

By 3:00 p.m., I was walking back to the car once again, this time with a large portion of clam chowder that I bought from a local eatery. Finley tasted his first clam that afternoon.

On our way home, I told him that we will come back to visit the point when a storm is lashing the shoreline. Why not? "We are nature junkies, m'boy."

Finley Savors a Bowser Beer and a Beefy Cigar

December 30, 2021

🐾

Is your dog drinking responsibly? Hops, alcohol and carbonation are not good for your dog. Keep the real beer for you and Bowser Beer for your pups! After all, someone has to be the designated walker.

—Bowser Beer for Dogs packaging

National Dog Day came and went without my having celebrated Finley. For a belated commemoration, I decided to order a Trio Sample Pack of Bowser Beer for Dogs, as well as a smoked beefy Bowser Cigar.

I know Finley and was positive that he would love them both.

Alcohol-free Bowser beers contain human-grade beef, chicken or pork and are combined with glucosamine for joint health; malt barley, which is packed full of vitamin B and amino acids, is also in each Bowser Beer.

I contacted Jenny Brown, the owner and founder of the Seattle-based company, to get the inside scoop. She described how many dog parents feel guilty after leaving their dog home alone all day. These parents will come home from work, wanting to be with their pup and include her/him in their evening's activities. Why not share a beer together?

Recent regulations in many West Coast cities have changed with regard to allowing pups to visit open-air bars and restaurants.

Humans and canines can now share happy hour together and more. Dog-friendly bars have proliferated; some even serve canines delicious meals such as the Woof-Woof Bowl, "a combination of beef, rice and power greens, topped with a sunny-side up and a coconut woof-woof sauce."

Ah, those West Coast ways! I wondered if Finley would share his meal with me under those circumstances.

Finley plopped down on the sofa next to me, a Beefy Brown Ale by his side. We began to watch the movie *Marley and Me*.

Finley is enjoying a Bowser Cigar.

This mostly true story is based on a Miami family who cared for and loved Marley, a yellow Labrador retriever, who, according to his parents, was "the world's worst dog."

Adorable, mischievous and often out-of-control, Marley failed obedience school.

Finley's eyes were fixed on the television, and he rose to his feet, upset, when he saw Marley destroying the household furniture. When Marley ran across the field from the left outfield corner to the right outfield corner between innings at a baseball game, while being chased by his parents, played by Jennifer Aniston and Owen Wilson, a roar of laughter and approval rose from the crowd who were unaware of what had really transpired.

My brother, ever the sports nut, is still proud to say that he was sitting behind home plate during this particular Brewers-Marlin's game that took place in May 2008.

Finley stood up once again and barked when he saw the aforementioned scene. Now panting and thirsty, Finley tried to swig his ale (his mom helped), but much of it trickled out of his mouth and ended up on the sofa. Then Finley smoked (ate) his banded cigar, which he found easier to do.

We wisely skipped the movie's finale; having seen it before, I knew that the ending would be excruciatingly sad.

Since Finley is a "feeler" and understands everything, I wanted him to be spared too.

At 5:00 p.m., I drizzled half a bottle of Finley's beer over his dinner chow. After finishing his delicious meal, he returned to his empty bowl multiple times, hoping for more.

Finley watching "Marley and Me" with a Bowser Beer by his side.

There are two more bottles of beer waiting for him in the fridge: a Porky Pup Porter and a Cock-a-Doodle Brew.

Little does he know.

PS. Finley and I want to wish you a happy and healthy 2022.

Three Adventures in Concord and Carlisle

January 6, 2022

🐾

The centerpiece of Punkatasset Preserve is Hutchins Pond, a man-made pond formed for harvesting winter ice to cool dairy products of the Hutchins Farm in days before refrigeration. Today the pond is inhabited by beavers and offers peaceful views. Above the pond stands Punkatasset Hill, a glacial drumlin, which on April 19, 1775, served as an observation post for Minutemen to observe British regulars advancing, leading to the battle at the Old North Bridge.
—Town of Concord, Punkatasset Preserve Trail Map and description of reserve

On a dreary, post-Thanksgiving morning, Finley and a human friend and I departed for Concord/Carlisle to visit a couple of nature preserves. I buckled Finley into his padded seat belt, and Finley and his gang were on our way. We passed a few attractive old farms, and I cracked open both of Finley's windows so he could smell the smells of this bucolic landscape. We reached the Elliot Concord River Preserve in Carlisle, located a few miles downriver from the Old North Bridge. From the high point of this property, we saw a scenic slice of the Concord River. We continued on the short 0.8-mile loop trail. Finley sped ahead and reached the river. He found a stick and ran around with it in the shallow water.

Our next stop was Estabrook Woods in Concord, "a well-regarded doggie destination," as described in a book about the best hikes to take with dogs in Boston and beyond. When I first visited the property about thirty years ago, the trails were not well mapped/marked, and Max, my first yellow Lab, and I got very lost in these twelve-hundred-acre woods. Since then, the Town of Concord created a new easy-to-follow map and put proper blazes at trail intersections.

Rather than hiking the loop trail around Hutchins Pond, we decided to climb the open-sided Punkatasset Hill. The sky had cleared, and the still warm sunshine declared that we sit down on the leaf-strewn grass partway up the hill. We watched a man run up and down the hill multiple times. After his fifth and final go-round, he told us that he was training for the coming ski season. Finley, admiring the man's fortitude, never barked at him. We continued on to the 289-foot summit. When there, we turned around to view Hutchins Pond in the distance.

Finley cavorts in the Concord River.

On the way home, I spontaneously decided to swing left into the parking lot of the Old North Bridge. After a brief walk, we reached the famous arched bridge, and I unleashed Finley; he ran toward the Concord River for the second time that day. I launched a stick that to my amazement flew one-third of the way across the river. Groups of people standing on the bridge were watching Finley swim for the stick; they cheered him on. In fact, one woman applauded him when he reached his prize. Finley took note. Pleased by the attention and now holding a super-sized stick in his mouth, Finley ran to greet his admirers when they stepped off the bridge. His powerful tail wagged hard as he ran over to greet each person, showing off his mighty stick. Joyful laughter came in waves when Finley swung around and through the growing crowd.

We followed the crowd back toward the parking lot. When we were about ready to cross the street, one woman standing next to me said, "He's really something, so proud!"

Indeed.

Finley and a friend are sitting on Punkatasset Hill.

I am looking at you. I am alert in the woods.

Finley Speaks!

January 13, 2022

🐾

Dogs do speak, but only to those who listen.
—Orhan Pamuk, *My Name Is Red*

Tomorrow is my third birthday. My mom is busy baking Tampa's Cinnamon Drops for my special day, while I am writing to you in her stead to tell you a few things about myself.

I was born in southern New Hampshire, the third boy in a litter of six puppies. I was born with an overbite, which probably would have required an expensive corrective surgery, so my breeder told my mom that she didn't have to adopt me; she could wait for another boy in a future litter of yellow pups. Luckily, my mom wanted me; she scooped me up in her arms and nuzzled my face and my small furry body. You know, I never needed that surgery. When I sleep on my back, though, my tongue slips out of my mouth, which is the one result of my overbite. I understand that I look quite silly.

My favorite job is being the four-legged security guard in my kingdom. As soon as I wake up in the morning, I race to the sunroom and alert my mom if I hear any noisy birds at the feeders.

Soon enough, my mom snaps on my new red 2022 collar and out we go. Now I begin my outdoor patrol. I track the smells of the animals that have trespassed in the nighttime, such as fox, coyote and deer, to name a few. The nerve of them!

I am a very lucky dog. I go on all kinds of adventures and meet many different dogs and humans along the way. Some dogs seem to be too shy or upset when I try to say hello. I do not understand why. I love living in the country and filling all my senses with the natural world. After hearing about the cacophonous sounds of the big cities' cars, taxis and ambulances, I know that I don't want to go there.

My mother talks to me a lot, and by now I understand her. When I stop to smell an interesting spot, she might exclaim such as, "Ah... to your nose, the scent of lilacs!"

Often she uses my name, which gets my attention, and I mostly comply with her requests or commands. I say "mostly" because when I am feeling mischievous, a little like Marley, I pretend that I am deaf to her calls. Unlike Marley, though, I have never destroyed the household furniture nor run across the field in a Major League Baseball game!

Sometimes when I lay chest-deep in thick mud, I turn into a black Lab. Although I relish swimming in frigid water, occasionally with icicles hanging down from my belly, I don't like being hosed down with cold water. I try to get away from it.

When my mom spoke to a friend about my incongruous behavior, her friend suggested that Mom add a hot-water spigot to possibly make it more comfortable for me. It worked. I am now okay with being sprayed with warm water and again turning back into a yellow Lab.

My mother tells me that I am a perfect de-stressor. When she wraps her arms around me, I can hear her slowing heartbeat and feel tension leaving her body; We look into each other's eyes with acknowledgment and much love. Mom says that increases the production of oxytocin, the love hormone. I am her large bundle of joy and she is my dear mom.

In short, I am strong, I am free and I love my life.

Finley Teaches Himself an Acrobatic Stick Game

January 20, 2022

🐾

Imagine lying down with headphones on, the words of "The Little Prince" floating through your ears. Then, the words are repeated in an unfamiliar language, followed by nonsense words. You're in an MRI machine, and inside your head, your brain is lighting up in response to the familiar and the unfamiliar. Oh, and you're a dog. When neuropathologist Laura Cuaya moved from Mexico to Hungary with her border collie, Kun-kun, she was driven to discover whether he could detect the language difference. The result: Cuaya's study of 18 dogs, monitored inside an MRI, demonstrated that the canine brain indeed recognized these changes. That makes dogs the first non-primates to possess spontaneous language ability. So, if you're streaming subtitled shows from other countries, Fido can tell."

—CNN World, January 10

Laura Cuaya's findings don't surprise me. We learn from a myriad of scientific studies, as well as our own observations, more and more about the abilities of our canine family members and friends.

Take Finley, for instance. We know that he loves to run around with the largest heaviest sticks available because that's what gives him much pleasure, some of it derived from solid human attention. What Finley can easily carry in his mouth is beyond belief; sometimes it is actually difficult for me to pick up one of his super sticks or tree limbs, as the case might be, and remove it from a forested path.

Finley taught himself a clever new game: how to hoist a favored stick up and over his neck and down his back.

The instructions for Finley's Acrobatic Stick Game are as follows:
1. With nose quivering, reach down to the ground and find the midpoint of a large stick that is resting perpendicular to your body.
2. With nose placed under this point, rear up, allowing the stick to slide down your snout while propelling it in such a way that it lands on the back of your neck still perpendicular to your body.
3. Allow the stick to slide down your back.
4. Just before it reaches your tail, and here comes the hard part, lower your head and sharply turn your neck around in order to transfer the stick onto the back of your neck before it falls off your tail.
5. Wait a couple of minutes, drop the stick, and repeat.

PS. Should you flub the sequence, keep practicing!
PPS. There are permutations and combinations to this game. Experiment.

On January 7, during our first snowfall of the season, Finley was playing another game. This time he was racing around in the approximate seven-inches of fresh powder with a new blue tennis ball that I had thrown out for him to find. The ball was one of six multicolored tennis balls that he received as a present for his third birthday. The ball sliced into the snow yards away. Just before reaching it and with a wild look in his eyes, Finley leaped into the air, back legs arching up, and pounced face first into the fluffy whiteness. Finley's nose knows. He retrieved it.

This game is hardly a Finley invention, though. Scenes of playful dogs scampering around and enjoying games in the snow are a many centuries-old tradition.

As Carl Zuckmayer, a German writer and playwright, informs us, "A life without a dog is a mistake."
So true.

The set-up

Finley Visits an Apple Orchard

February 3, 2022

🐾

An old British custom with regard to apples goes as follows: "On Christmas Eve the farmers and their men in Devonshire take a large bowl of cider with a toast in it, and carrying it in state to the orchard, they salute the apple trees with much ceremony in order to make them bear well the next season."

This salutation consists of "throwing some of the cider about the roots of the tree, placing bits of the toast on the branches," and then "encircling one of the best bearing trees in the orchard, they drink the following toast three times":

Here's to thee, old apple tree,

Whence thou mayst bud, and whence thou mayst blow,

And whence thou mayst bear apples enow!

Hats full! Caps full!

Bushel, bushel, sacks full!

And my pockets full, too! Hurra!

—John Brand, *Brand's Popular Antiquities of Great Britain*

The outdoor temperature rose to fourteen degrees on the day before we went to Honey Pot Hill Orchards in Stow.

On the day before that, an arctic blast gave us a windchill of approximately ten degrees below zero, the coldest day in three years. Finley and I were well prepared; Finley wore his natural inner and outer coats while I was wearing a super down-filled jacket, the one that I had purchased at an REI garage sale about twenty years ago.

The snow at the Gray Reservation in Sudbury had partially melted from some days of above freezing temperature and then refroze when the temperature dipped below thirty-two degrees. The resulting ice was also deeply rutted from footprints from the earlier snow. Despite wearing steel-coiled ice walkers, I found myself sliding on some of the patches of ice. Finley was slip sliding away as well. We were quite the pair that morning.

The walking conditions required my heavier duty mini crampons, which of course were sitting on a shelf back home.

"Finley, let's get out of here and drive over to Honey Pot," I declared; "We'll avoid the ice and make the first tracks in the rows of snow between the apple trees!" Within fourteen minutes Finley was racing up one row and down another. Occasionally he turned around to see if I was following him.

Crab apples, wild apples, and cultivated apples are a wonderful part of our New England heritage. In 1860, Henry David Thoreau wrote an essay entitled "Wild Apples." He said, "The cultivated apple was first introduced into this country by the earliest settlers, and is thought to do as well or better here than anywhere else. Probably some of the varieties which are now cultivated were first introduced into Britain by the Romans."

Finley and I needed to resupply our stock of our favored Macoun apples. Crisp and somewhat sweet, at least to my palate, Prairie (the horse) loves these apples as well.

When I once presented her with a tart Cortland apple, she turned her nose away. Sweet apples for a sweet horse. Prairie loves her quartered Macouns with a side of three to four peppermint candies.

Since Finley and I found ourselves alone in the refrigerated apple shop, I unleashed him, thinking that he wouldn't be interested in unlawfully taking an apple off the shelf unless of course it were to be topped with a dollop of peanut butter.

In that I was correct. Instead, Finley came bounding around a corner of the shop with a large dog cookie in the shape of a moose. His tail whipped back and forth, his eyes sheepishly asking me, *Please*. I added his moose to my basket.

Before we reached the nonexistent cashier, I posed the happy pup in front of four levels of step-up shelves containing bags of Spencer apples. I read that this variety is slightly tart, but I can't really say. Since the honor system prevails at this time of year at Honey Pot, I added my twenty dollars to the pile of other bills on the counter.

On the way home we stopped at a roadside pull off adjacent to the Assabet River. Finley ate his moose while I enjoyed my juicy apple. I turned on the radio, and we listened to Senate Majority Leader Chuck Schumer eulogize Senator Harry Reid, who was lying in state in the rotunda of the US Capitol building: "A quiet voice, but filled with thunder …"

Finley poses in front of the Spencer apple shelves.

Finley Inspects Upper Mill Brook

February 10, 2022

🐾

    The storms called nor'easters usually bring strong northeast winds over the east as they move along the Atlantic coast. Nor'easters bring heavy rain, heavy snow and severe coastal flooding. A nor'easter can be a blizzard or vice versa. A blizzard, though, has a specific meteorological definition according to the National Weather Service: A storm that has blowing and/or falling snow with winds of at least 35mph, which reduces visibilities to a quarter of a mile or less for at least 3 hours. In popular usage, however, the term is used for any heavy snowstorm accompanied by strong winds. A bomb cyclone, another event, can rival, in some aspects, the intensity of strong hurricanes in the Atlantic. A bomb cyclone is essentially a winter hurricane.
    —Apple News and 1440 Daily Digest, January 31

On this historic day, January 29, Massachusetts experienced all three meteorological events: a nor'easter, a blizzard and a bomb cyclone. Luckily, Finley and I didn't lose power or have a tree fall on our house as had occurred in the blizzard of March 18, ten months before Finley was born.

The day after the storm dawned sunny and cold. Finley was tucked into my lap as I was engaged in my breath-work practice. Suddenly, sunlight came in through a gap in the White Pines; it was as if "the sun poured in like butterscotch and stuck to all my senses" (an imaginative line from Joni Mitchell's song "Chelsea Morning"). Finley's light cream-colored shoulder patches, essentially angel wings, were illuminated by the light. The soul of a sunbeam on Finley's smooth coat!

We were on our way to Upper Mill Brook in Wayland because the area contains a mixture of forest, fields and little ponds worthy of exploration. Finley was sitting in the backseat of the car watching people as they were shoveling or snow-blowing their driveways; the great cleanup had begun. Finley broke trail, his shoulders strong and supple as he leaped through the snow. I followed him on snowshoes.

Then he decided to follow me, inadvertently stepping on the backs of my snowshoes and causing me to tumble forward into the powdery snow. Oh, Finley! We followed our noses, not paying attention to the trail markers since we were Upper Mill Brook's first visitors.

I reasoned that we could follow our own tracks back to the parking lot. And eventually we did. During the last few minutes of our outing, we saw a cross-country skier making her own kind of tracks near the shore of Benjamin Pond. She was kicking and gliding in perfect form, magnificent to behold.

With a salmon treat almost ready, I called Finley back as he was on his way to giving her one of his oh-so-friendly greetings.

I wanted to prevent him from stepping on her skis and you know the rest.

The crisp winter air, the magic of a landscape covered with glistening snow and the antics of a happy pup were offered that morning. I delivered a silent thank you in return. Finley enjoyed himself immensely too, but then again, he always does.

Finley stretches out to reach a stick.

Finley is bounding through the snow.

Finley Participates in a Game of Mental Stimulation

February 24, 2022

Dogs are incredibly smart and intuitive, so, just like humans, in addition to daily physical exercise, their minds need to be exercised each day to help them tap into their true potential and maintain their overall health. In addition to cognitive improvements, the right balance of physical and mental exercise can improve your dog's mood. Dogs thrive when they have jobs to do, so giving their brain a quick workout each day keeps them satisfied and happy.

—happypuppytips.com

Finley passed his physical exam with flying colors. After losing eight pounds, Dr. Susan Rabaut found him to be in excellent physical shape. "Is there anything else I can do to keep the pup happy?" I queried. "Mental stimulation would be good for him," she replied.

It was snowing lightly that morning. Today, I was going to stimulate Finley's mind, or so I had hoped. We were going to play the canine version of hide and seek. Prior to starting the game, I wanted to engage Finley in a game of fetch with the oversized tennis ball that he had received for his third birthday.

The ball landed in an open space behind the pine trees; Tito and Abby, my Suffolk sheep, were grazing, snow blanketing their coats. Finley ignored them. Tito, the larger of the two sheep, arrived in a big box from Plow and Hearth. Tito, a resin garden statue, was delivered instead of the metal bench that I had ordered.

"Keep the sheep, we'll send you the bench," declared the company's representative when I called. Then Tito beget Abby, his darling little daughter. But that's another story!

About twenty minutes passed before I walked into the back woods looking for a broad tree to hide behind. Before I was properly situated, Finley ran up to me, wondering about this new happening. I picked up the tennis ball that he had dropped and hurled it deeper into the woods, while I tiptoed over to another tree that was wide enough to conceal me. Finley was upon me in a flash; this occurrence once again was not the goal of the game. Soon Finley became preoccupied with his just-found soccer ball; he raced off, being highly adept at nosing his ball through the trees.

Now I had my chance. I found a third tree and secured my place behind it, barely breathing. I whispered, "Finley, oh Finley." And again. I remained there convinced that he could hear me above the sounds of his play. Under the circumstances, he was supposed to find me to successfully complete his first round of mental exercise.

I peeked out from behind the tree. There he was not thirty feet away and looking up at the sky. Again, I whispered, "Finley, oh Finley." He never attempted to find me, though I remained standing there for a few more minutes. During those minutes, I too looked upward and considered the sky.

Another birthday gift that Finley received was Outward Hound, a dog-twister game. The goal (as stated on the packaging) is to "unlock, slide and find hidden treats."

No need to wish you luck, Fin; You'll do just fine.

Finley is playing near Tito

Covered Bridges and Great Friends in Vermont

March 17, 2022

🐾

While dogs hate loud noises, they love soft music. Just like humans, music can also be soothing to them. But each dog has his or her own preference. This means that you have to discover your dog's favorite sounds. Reggae or soft rock is usually the preferred music of dogs.
—Happy Puppy Tips, happypuppytips.com

A wonderful invitation came our way! We were going to spend a few days in central Vermont, sharing adventures with Finley's best friend Bo and his parents.

They had rented a house with an expansive front yard that would provide a perfect doggy playscape, not to mention a nice view of Mount Ascutney in the background.

After packing Finley's X-large black L.L. Bean canvas tote, I chose some of my favorite reggae music for our driving pleasure, one of which was a Putumayo collection of Jamaica's reggae sounds.

Though the word buffeted is more akin to battered, Finley and Bo buffeted one another in the intense pleasure of their reunion. They continued to play hard throughout their four days together.

"Since we're so close to Woodstock, let's walk through a couple of their covered bridges," I suggested.

Twenty minutes later, Finley and Bo were standing in front of Middle Bridge that spans the Ottauquechee River. The span is the first truly authentic road covered bridge in New Hampshire or Vermont since 1895.

The pups ran along the pedestrian walkway on their first covered bridge in Vermont.

I could have told Finley about the night of the Fireman's Ball, back in May of 1974, when the bridge was set on fire by a group of local youths, causing destruction of the roof and siding and extensive damage elsewhere, but I didn't.

I didn't speak of the thousands of dollars that were retrieved by court order, garnishing a percentage of the wages of those perpetrators old enough to work.

We left Middle Bridge and continued on to visit the picturesque, barn-red Taftsville Covered Bridge that was built in 1838, making it the third oldest bridge in the state.

To my mind, Vermont is the most dog-friendly state in the United States.

For example, most of the shops in Woodstock lay out the red carpet for pups and their owners, providing dog biscuits, water and warm welcomes.

Smiles abounded when Finley and Bo entered the Vermont Flannel Company shop.

The boys cozied up to a life-size, plush chocolate Lab while the humans contemplated the brochure's age-old question: "Where have all your flannels gone?"

Finley and Bo are standing in front of Middle Bridge in Woodstock, Vermont.

The humans responded, each restocking with a pair of the softest, thickest pajama/lounge pants imaginable.

The following morning we enjoyed a hike that looped around Pogue Lake near Woodstock.

The snow was fresh, the day was clear and at thirty-seven degrees was warm for a mid-February day. And, oh, that sapphire sky!

Quechee Gorge, a legacy of the ice age, is always worth viewing or hiking. The gorge is 165-feet deep and over a mile in length.

We hiked partway down from the Route 4 Bridge overlooking the gorge; unexpectedly, we came across a dam that was built to provide power for a clothing mill that manufactured material used to make baseball uniforms for the Boston Red Sox and the New York Yankees. Imagine that.

Finley and I could have stayed in the Green Mountain State for several days; there was much more to experience. Additionally, Finley and Bo were not at all ready to say their goodbyes.

Vermont does it better.

Finley and Bo together again, this time in central Vermont.

184

Making Friends on a Walk along Hop Brook

March 24, 2022

🐾

Laughter connects you with people. It's almost impossible to maintain any kind of distance or any sense of social hierarchy when you're just howling with laughter. Laughter is a force for democracy.

—John Cleese

March 10: Woke up to two inches of wet snow, a "nuisance" storm, as described by one weather forecaster. Walked with a dear friend from Hawaii who had not seen a snowstorm in fifty years, down by the big bridge in Hop Brook, thirty-seven degrees with great gobs of snow falling on our heads. My friend was mesmerized by the magical landscape, and Finley swam hard beneath the bridge. The snow will be gone by nightfall.

March 12: Finley and I turned right when we left our driveway, wheeling into the gray of the morning. Within four minutes, we were driving along the lane that would again lead us to Hop Brook.

A tree had fallen on the footpath which Finley easily leaped over. Minutes later Mazie, a year-old yellow Lab pup, sprinted over to greet Finley. He took to her right away. The party grew when Finley and Mazie met a pair of golden retrievers who were coming toward us from the opposite direction; one of them was an eleven-month-old puppy and the other an eleven-year-old senior citizen. Watching them play together, I ventured, "We could start a doggie day camp here and now." There were no takers.

Like Finley, Mazie is an unmitigated stick-o-maniac who loves to run. Finley even "runs" in his sleep; his legs will dart back and forth, and I know that he is having a blast. Likely, Mazie does the same.

By the time we reached the bank before the big bridge, Finley and Mazie were engaged in a tug of war on their shared stick. Being much larger and stronger than Mazie, Finley was able to tear the stick out of her mouth 100 percent of the time. Out of politeness, he did relinquish his stick to her once. But only once.

While the aforementioned was taking place, Rui appeared on the scene. He is an almost two-year-old mix of an Australian cattle dog and a coonhound. Because of his Australian heritage, his parents had thought of naming him kangaroo which became shortened to Ru. Then came the tender diminutive of the name: he became Rui.

By this time, Finley and Mazie had taken their game into Hop Brook. Standing at the edge of the water, Rui became the designated lifeguard.

Now sticks began flying through the air and into the water while the two retrievers swam hard to get each one of them. With one exception, the humans were hilariously and hopelessly rooting for Mazie.

Finley and I may never again cross paths with these lovely dogs and their parents, but what fun it was while it lasted.

Rui is the lifeguard. He is an almost two-year-old Australian cattle dog and coonhound mix.

Finley and Mazie are engaged in a tug of war.

Finley is looking down the beach.

Finley enjoys digging on Crane Beach.

Playing in the White Sand at Crane Beach in Ipswich

March 31, 2022

🐾

No matter how much time passes, no matter what takes place in the interim, there are some things we can never assign to oblivion, memories we can never rub away.
—Haruki Murakami

"Finley, we have a deadline, that's if you want to walk on three great beaches on the north shore," I declared. He looked up, interested.

"Yes," I continued, "you're not even allowed to *step* on those beaches from April 15 through October 15, so we've got to go soon!"

Unparalleled Crane Beach in Ipswich would be the focus of today's adventure; it is four miles of a white-sand barrier beach which helps anchor a coastal system that includes a thousand acres of sand dunes and maritime forest. The land is managed by The Trustees of Reservations, Massachusetts' largest conservation and preservation organization. Crane Beach is shallow with a graduated drop, so when the tide goes out, the water is relatively warm.

The Trustees' ranger, sitting in his ATV, was driving around the parking lot looking for recent four-legged arrivals. Part of his job is to recite the beach rules: Dogs are allowed to be off leash to the left of the yellow pole, which is on the left-hand side of the beach. Pickup bags are available at a station near the kiosk.

Locating the pole was somewhat of a challenge, though, because the yellow paint had almost completely faded.

Holding onto his new tennis ball, Finley ran out to investigate the sand beneath the outgoing tide. There, he dropped his ball onto the wet sand and then began digging. With front legs extended, he flung the sand surrounding his ball backward until the ball fell into one of the hollows made by his digging, and then the ball partially disappeared. He excavated his prize, and with a wild look in his eye ran down the beach, eventually dropping the ball only to begin his solo game anew.

Facing northeast, I looked up the coast to see the town of Ipswich and Plum Island in the near distance. The Isles of Shoals in New Hampshire and horse: the southern coast of Maine were hidden beneath a bank of low-lying clouds.

Crane Beach is among the world's most important nesting sites for piping plovers, a threatened bird that was nearly hunted to extinction in the nineteenth century for its eggs and feathers. Snowy owls who migrate from the Arctic nest in the dunes as well.

Finley and I walked parallel to the dunes soon after we crossed back into the "leashed" section of the beach. Finley was not happy with this turn of events. Suddenly we became distracted by some distant creatures that were running towards us. At first glance they appeared to be camels. Finley stood and stared. He didn't bark when a line of horses and their riders thundered past us. Apparently, this was the section of the beach that allowed for unleashed horses.

Finley and I turned around, starting the walk back towards his section of the beach. Free again, he stayed close to the water's edge, continuing to exult in his unaccompanied play. He paid no attention to the poodle that passed by. He was way too busy.

A Visit to Singing Beach in Manchester-by-the-Sea

April 7, 2022

🐾

Singing Beach's unusual name comes from the unusual qualities of its sand: under the right conditions, it resonates when walked upon, creating a squeaking or creaking noise. The so-called "singing" is a phenomenon created by sand of a certain size, shape and make-up when it is disturbed. It can make a rather loud squeaking sound!

—northshoremag.com

Hi ho, hi ho, it's off to the beach we go.

On the morning of the vernal equinox, March 20, we decided to continue with part two of our beach adventures on the North Shore.

Clear and sunny to start, an abrupt line of dense fog enveloped us twenty minutes before we reached our destination. The temperature dropped nine degrees to a still very pleasant fifty-eight degrees.

I was surprised to see that the fog had mostly dissipated by the time we stood evaluating the beach fanning out before us. My jaw dropped. Dozens of unleashed pups, the crowd mostly made up of large and giant breeds, were running or swimming for balls that were thrown out for them. Instantly, Finley ran out to retrieve a tennis ball that was meant for a Greyhound. After two attempts to outrace him, Finley gave up, smart pooch that he is.

Unlike 4-mile-long Crane Beach that was featured in last week's column, Singing Beach is a compact, crescent shaped half-mile long beach. There are expansive views of rugged shoreline, rocky islands and the open ocean, reminding me of the Maine coast.

Finley and his soccer companion race for the ball.

With a burning question in mind, I approached two local teenagers: "Have you ever heard the sand singing?"

"Yes," said one, "sometimes I hear a squeaking sound, and the best chance of hearing that is to walk on the dry sand above the tide line."

Meanwhile, dogs were continuing to arrive in droves, their senses absorbing the sight, sound and smells of the beach and of pups frolicking on it. I kept an eye on Finley as I shuffled barefoot along the dry sand and listened for squeaking, creaking, singing, humming or whistling sounds. There were none. Perhaps the sound of the surf or the sound waves bouncing back and forth beneath the sand from all the running and swimming creatures had something to do with it.

I caught sight of a human soccer player expertly maneuvering his ball along the tide line. Finley had not as yet met another soccer player. As they practiced together, Finley navigated the ball to the left and right, away from his opponent, twenty-year-old Nabil, who tried to regain control of the ball.

Nabil grinned throughout the entire time he spent with Finley. By now, a few people had gathered, watching Finley and Nabil play; they were laughing, pointing and taking pictures of the energetic duo.

Not remotely tired, Nabil took a thirty-second water break, while Finley refused to drink the cold

Soccer moves

water that I poured into his collapsible travel water bowl. He was evidently impatient for the game to begin once again.

The better part of the day was behind us; it was time to leave the beach. Nabil put his arms around Finley's neck and gave him a hug. Then he said to me, "I hope that Finley continues his career as a soccer star!"

Indubitably.

Having a Ball on Wingaersheek Beach in Gloucester

April 14, 2022

🐾

Crafted in 1923, in honor of Gloucester's 300th anniversary, the Memorial To The Gloucester Fishermen is an 8-foot bronze statue of a fisherman standing braced at the wheel on the sloping deck of his ship. It is positioned so that the fisherman is looking out over Gloucester Harbour. The fisherman in the statue was modeled after captain Clayton Morrissey, a prominent Gloucester fisherman. The fisherman was posed to look as if he was facing a windstorm and was headed toward dangerous rocks. On the harbor side of the base is an inscription that reads: "THEY THAT GO DOWN TO THE SEA IN SHIPS 1623–1923."

—Wikipedia.com

Good morning, Gloucester!

Painted on the glass of the kiosk fronting the short path to Wingaersheek Beach is an admonition that reads: "Putting dog poop in a bag and not taking it with you is a sign of mental deficiency."

"Wow, Finley, what a cool sign," I said in reaction to it. When we reached the beach, Finley ran to the left, attracted by a golden retriever that was lying in the sand beneath her mom, who was sitting in a naturally formed seat in an attractive rock formation.

Finley made three play bows before he realized that he couldn't entice Hannah Jumper from Rockport to play with him. Intrigued, I asked about the origin of the pup's name. In the mid-nineteenth century, as the story goes, Hannah Jumper from Rockport, chief organizer of the temperance movement in Rockport, became sick of the multitudes of townsmen passed out in the streets, intoxicated by rum. With a group of women, Hannah's "Hatchet Gang" raided Rockport's stockpile of alcohol, smashing and hatcheting their way through all the kegs in town. I later learned that on that day Rockport was described as a colossal punch bowl, "with which the smell of rum drifted for two miles across the bay." Because of Hannah's success, Rockport became a dry town till 2005.

Finley has a blast at Wingaersheek Beach in Gloucester.

Wingaersheek Beach's low tide goes on forever. Huge rocks, perfect for climbing, interspersed with numerous tide pools were sources of wonderment for the yellow pup.

Finley met a goldendoodle, also named Finley. They had a blast running and splashing together through the tide pools. When I called out for Finley to return to me, both Finleys came running.

We continued with our walk, leaving humans and pups behind. By this time Finley had lost his tennis ball, and there were no sticks to be had. I didn't know how to react to his questioning eyes. I threw my hands up and said to him, "I really don't know, Finley!"

Entrepreneur that he is, Finley soon found a spot in the sand and began a deep dig; he unearthed a large blackened log that had graced a former bonfire. I sat down on the sand nearby, closed my eyes and began to slowly breathe in the bright April sunshine.

Suddenly, a pile of wet sand, forcefully flung back from Finley's big paws, hit me squarely in the face. I screeched. Finley was shocked and moved away from me. I closed my eyes again and resumed the practice, only to be hit in the face once more by flying sand. Additionally, the incoming tide caught me by surprise—the water reached up to the seat of my pants. No longer could I sit like the Buddha!

Finley and I left the beach, wet and sandblasted. We proceeded to drive over to the Gloucester Fisherman's Memorial statue to pay our respects to the over 5,300 fisherman (prior to 1923) who died at sea.

Though I could see that Finley was a little on the tired side after his 2 1/2 hour romp on the beach, we still made our way over to one of the arms of huge Gloucester harbor to watch the fishing boats. Many of them were heading out to sea to catch scallops during the fishermen's month-long allowance. Finley and I stood at the end of the pier watching the gulls fly from one post to another. Some of the many pleasures of the harbor.

Gloucester's four-hundredth anniversary, a year-long celebration, will take place next year. Finley and I intend to book a pet-friendly accommodation, if only to watch the greasy pole, capture the flag contest when all the participants tumble into the sea with only one of them having captured the flag.

Finley sniffs an abandoned lobster trap.

A Visit to Rocky Woods and Rocky Narrows

April 21, 2022

🐾

There is such strength in the ground, the trees, the water. The air we breathe washes over us with new life. Water is drawn into the atmosphere and returns to fill rivers and streams. The mountains rise up, are worn away, and rise again. On the high tundra tiny flowers bloom unseen. The cycle of the seasons is alive with the promise of rebirth.
—*Daily Meditations* by **Martha Whitmore Hickman**

Rocky Narrows and Rocky Woods: the upper basin of the Charles River, Chickering Pond and lots of very large rocks.

Rocky Narrows in Sherborn is picturesque, with an outstanding view of the Charles River from hundred-feet-high King Philip's Overlook.

I remember that view.

In the autumn of 1991, I picnicked there with my first yellow Lab puppy, Max. He was a big-headed, warm-hearted and intelligent boy like Finley.

Finley, friends and I stood atop King Philip's Overlook, a 650-million-year-old rock cliff, admiring early spring views of the budding trees and the Charles River.

Steep wooded banks rose from both sides of the river, forming a narrow passageway, hence the name Rocky Narrows.

Kaio throws a stick in Rocky Woods.

Finley explored every inch of the broad rock face. I whirled into a daydream, seeing him pick up scents from the year 1676, when King Philip, the English name given to Metacomet, sachem of the Wampanoag tribe during the time of King Philip's War, stood here scouting the countryside for his enemy, the English settlers.

I was drawn back to the present when I sensed new activity. Four older teens walked out onto the relatively flat rock and sat down.

Finley, ever the greeter, drew peals of laughter as he ran around them. One young man started talking to Finley and drew him in.

"You need a dog." I found myself saying.

"I don't have a say. If I could, I'd get five," he replied.

Reluctantly, we left the overlook, not having seen the red-tailed hawks that frequent this area.

We continued walking the short loop trail that led us back to the parking area. My friends departed for home, while Finley and I continued on to visit Rocky Woods in Medfield, another property managed by The Trustees of Reservations.

There, Finley could swim in Chickering Pond, the largest of the reservation's five man-made ponds.

Our plan was to walk the three-quarter-mile loop around the pond. Nicely spaced picnic tables located at the water's edge had wide-open views of the pond. Finley picked up a rather large stick and ran headlong into the pond, happy to be back in his element.

At the same time that Fin was swimming back to shore with his stick, I saw a stick flying over my head and into the water.

Immediately, Finley reversed course, swimming back to retrieve it. I turned around as well to see a laughing family of three: Flavio, his wife Claudiana and their thirteen-year-old son Kaio. Finley beamed as a parade of sticks were hurled out into the pond.

The Brazilian family called out their enthusiasm and excitement with words spoken in both Brazilian Portuguese and English.

Altogether now, we resumed our walk around the pond. Sticks were still flying through the air, arcing over the path or into the water. And so it was for the rest of our fabulous walk together.

Hours later, I emailed the days photos to Flavio. He replied: "hey, thank you very much. We are happy to meet you. Finley is amazing."

The pleasure is mine.

Finley is standing on King Philip's Rock in Rocky Narrows.

A Bit of a Misadventure at Elm Bank Reservation

April 28, 2022

Finley cannot get out of the Charles River by himself.

I was young and foolish then; now I am older and foolisher.
—Mark Twain

The meandering Charles River flows from its source in Hopkinton for 78.3 miles, descending to Boston Harbor. People have lived along the Charles River for at least 9000 years.

I told Finley that he would experience his first swim in the Charles River today. That would occur at mile marker thirty-nine, the location of the quite fantastic Elm Bank Reservation, a Massachusetts Horticultural Society property. We were going for a walk with our new Brazilian friends, the ones that we met in Rocky Woods some weeks ago.

Finley's friend Flavio hoists him out of the river

We parked, circuiting the parking lot on foot, and waited for them to arrive. We tried to make contact but with no luck.

Finley couldn't believe that he was walking around a parking lot when instead he could have been liberated to run, swim, jump or fly into the Charles River, which he undoubtedly smelled.

The reservation is on a peninsula surrounded on three sides by the river. Pups who obey voice commands are allowed off leash everywhere except for in the multi-themed gardens or on the ball fields. Finley and I gave those gardens and ball fields a wide berth.

Now off leash, Finley belted forward on the Riverside Loop Trail. Within minutes we heard excited calls of "Finley, Finley, Finley." We whipped around to see our friends running toward us. Jumping for joy, Finley began to run around in circles, which he often does when he feels especially happy or proud.

What happened next could possibly be described as Finley's first misadventure. Still excited from his heartfelt reunion, Finley spotted an orange ball floating in the current; he ran down the long embankment and flew into the water to retrieve it. When he was ready to come ashore, he could not. The river bank was too steep. He stretched out his long frame to heave himself up and over the seventy-five-degree natural bank. Finley began to whimper. While rolling up my pants to prepare myself for his rescue, I called out to reassure him, "Everything's gonna be okay, Finley!"

Flavio reached Finley first. After a few attempts, Flavio was able to hoist the yellow pup out of the river.

Finley was not in any danger, though. Had Flavio not been with us, and had I not been strong enough to haul Finley out of the water myself, we would have made our way along the shoreline until we found an easier means of exiting the river.

Though I didn't see how it happened, I saw Finley's orange ball rolling down the embankment and into the water. *Huh?* I thought.

"It's my turn now," I loudly declared, but Flavio, forty years my junior, won the competition again, lifting eighty-eight pound Finley out of the Charles. I pictured members of the Wampanoag tribe, who had lived along these shores, laughing as hard as we did. This incident marked Finley's introduction to the noble Charles River.

It began to rain heavily. Finley thought nothing of it. He couldn't have known that I had left my rain jacket behind in our car.

We ran much of the way back, and I felt "once more the pulse's stirring play."

Visiting Cowassock Woods and Ashland Town Forest

May 5, 2022

🐾

The fire hydrant is taller than Finley

The single biggest thing that I learned was from an indigenous elder of Cherokee descent, Stan Rushworth, who reminded me of the difference between a Western settler mindset of "I have rights" and an indigenous mindset of "I have obligations." Instead of thinking that I am born with rights, I choose to think that I am born with obligations to serve past, present and future generations, and the planet herself.

—Etv and Farooq Chuhan

In preparation for the following Finley adventure, I joined the Sudbury Valley Trustees' guided meander through some of the many trails of Cowassock Woods and the Ashland Town Forest. I thought this a great way to celebrate Earth Day '22. A partnership had been formed between SVT and the town of Ashland to protect and preserve Cowassock Woods and the adjoining Ashland Town Forest, thus forming a tract of 700 acres. I was pleased to see the debut of the Forest Health Audio Tour, created by SVT. As one faces each QR code mounted on a wooden post, a narrator provides interesting information about the forest and its residents.

I couldn't wait to bring Finley to these woods for his belated Earth Day romp!

Immediately, he started running through an area known as "Invasive Alley." Invasives are non-native, aggressive plants that grow faster than native species and are far less nutritious for wildlife. I saw stands of the awful glossy buckthorn and Asiatic bittersweet vines climbing and strangling trees. Invasives thrive where the forest has been cleared or at the very least, disturbed.

Finley poses by an abandoned car in Cowassock Woods in Framingham.

Finley and I passed a few standing dead trees (snags) which, on the positive side, provide habitat for birds, bats and other wildlife. We have seen chickadees fly out from a cavity in one of the snags in our own backyard. Many birds build nests in these protected cavities.

We stopped to listen to the loud pecking of a Pileated woodpecker on a tall snag, in search of carpenter ants to eat. Those unmistakable sounds never fail to get our attention. Measuring sixteen to nineteen inches in length, the Pileated woodpecker is the third largest living species of woodpecker in the world.

Finley and I crossed the bridge that spanned bubbling Cowassock Brook. A large clump of Marsh marigolds (glossy yellow) stood in the wetland, a perfect visual bouquet for our walk.

From snags in the woods to a circa 1950s/early '60s abandoned car in the woods.

That must have been some party, I thought. Finley dashed over to investigate the rusted-out vehicle; he didn't stop to greet the man who was reaching into it, taking many photos of the car's interior.

"Why are you taking photos?" I asked. His wife loves old cars but was unable to be with him today. "This car's a passion project," he intoned. "I think she's way beyond that," I replied.

Fin and I left the corroded car behind and came across another anomaly, this time a fire hydrant located about forty feet off the path. We made our way over to it. Rob St. Germain, yesterday's group co-leader and SVT steward of these woods, told the group about a thirty-five-acre development that was slated to be built here where Finley and I presently stood. But the developers could not go forward with their project due to SVT's efforts to protect and preserve the land.

"At least we'll have water in case of a forest fire!" Rob said.

Needless to say, invasives were evident here, too.

I didn't mention that families fleeing the horror of the Salem Witch Trials of 1692-1693 sought refuge in this wilderness; they lived in collapsed caves in the Ashland Town Forest.

Just before leaving the woods, I told Finley that we are definitely going to explore those caves when we return.

Finley wagged his tail, looked up at me and smiled.

Visiting Coney Island in Brooklyn, New York

May 12, 2022

🐾

    Coney Island was once the largest amusement area in the country at the turn of the 20th Century and was famed for its technological innovations at the time such as electric lights, roller coasters as well as a showcase of the world's most bizarre sideshows.

—Google.com

Finley's Adventures debuted on May 14, 2020, with an article entitled "Meet Finley." For the second anniversary of the publication of his column, Finley and I planned an extra special adventure; we were going to Coney Island in Brooklyn, New York, to spend the day with his four young cousins. Since Finley knows them through visits and FaceTime, excitement abounded as he surged through my sister's apartment door in Manhattan. A rousing game of jumping from bed to bed began in earnest.

While Coney Island was one of my favorite childhood stomping grounds, Finley, Blake, Ella, Kivi, and Zazie hadn't yet experienced the thrills of being on some of the over fifty rides and competing in other attractions. The children tested their strength on a game where everyone, including Finley, won a small plush animal, given for his excellent conduct and so that he wouldn't feel left out.

Finley is staring at the Skee-ball

Carnival barkers called out to gain Finley's attention, while dispensing compliments: "Oh, how handsome," or "He's so friendly!" Dressed as a leopard, one barker wanted to have a photograph taken with Finley. The yellow pup was puzzled but unafraid of all the oddities that he encountered.

We queued up for a spin on the Wonder Wheel, standing in the line that would deposit us into one of the non-swaying white cars. Just before it was our turn to ride, I asked the ride's operator about Sunny, the twelve-year-old rottweiler who guards the property by night and who rides in white car number four by day. "Some people think it's funny, some people think it's cruel, but the dog thinks otherwise. We do it because she likes it," said long-term wheel operator Andrew Crowley to the *Daily News*.

Today's operator didn't speak English, so I asked my question in Spanish, "Sunny, el perro, esta aqui hoy?" (Sunny, the dog, is he here today?) The operator didn't entertain my question but instead pointed Finley and the gang to the right car. We reached the apex of the Wonder Wheel and saw the skyline of Manhattan, thirteen miles away as the crow flies.

When we began to play a game of Skee-Ball in the arcade, Finley couldn't contain himself. He jumped up onto the inclined lane and ran after the ball. That might have been the first event of its kind in the history of Coney Island. Finley stopped to watch a man shooting hoops. Skee-Balls, basketballs—Finley stared at them all in wonder.

Next, Finley and I boarded the carousel and sat on its bench together, while the children rode on gloriously painted horses. Finley and I shared an all-beef hot dog at Nathan's original hot dog stand, founded by a Polish immigrant in 1916. I didn't put mustard and sauerkraut on Finley's half, though.

The warm and beautiful weather called for a stroll along Coney Island's famous boardwalk. There are so many "famous" attractions in Coney Island.

I would be remiss if I didn't mention the Cyclone, now the second steepest roller coaster in the world. I could hear excited and/or terrified screams as the roller coaster made its way around its course.

Before we left the Isle of Coney, Finley walked down the few steps to the beach and enjoyed a short but enjoyable swim in the Atlantic Ocean.

Finley is looking at the basketball

Finley and I stood alone on the corner of Seventy-Second Street and First Avenue in Manhattan. Finding neither grass nor woods, he found it impossible to do his business on the concrete sidewalks of New York. When he looked up at me, I sensed his confusion. Not too long after we crossed the Triborough Bridge aka the RFK Bridge, we found a large grass patch for him.

"We had a great day with the kiddos, Finley. Now it's time to return to the country. By the way, *congratulations* on the successful completion of your ninety-eighth adventure. Peace and love, dear boy, I couldn't have done it without you!"

Additional Images of Finley

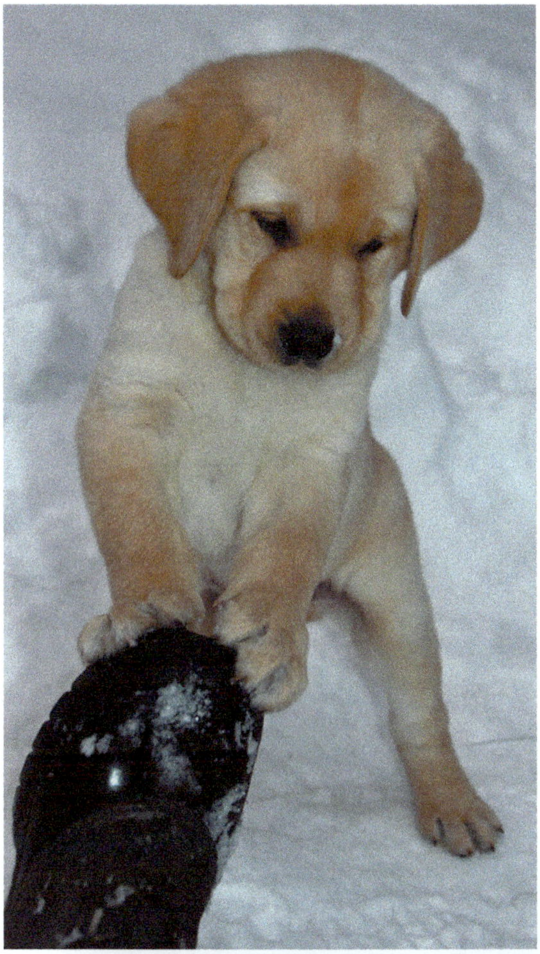

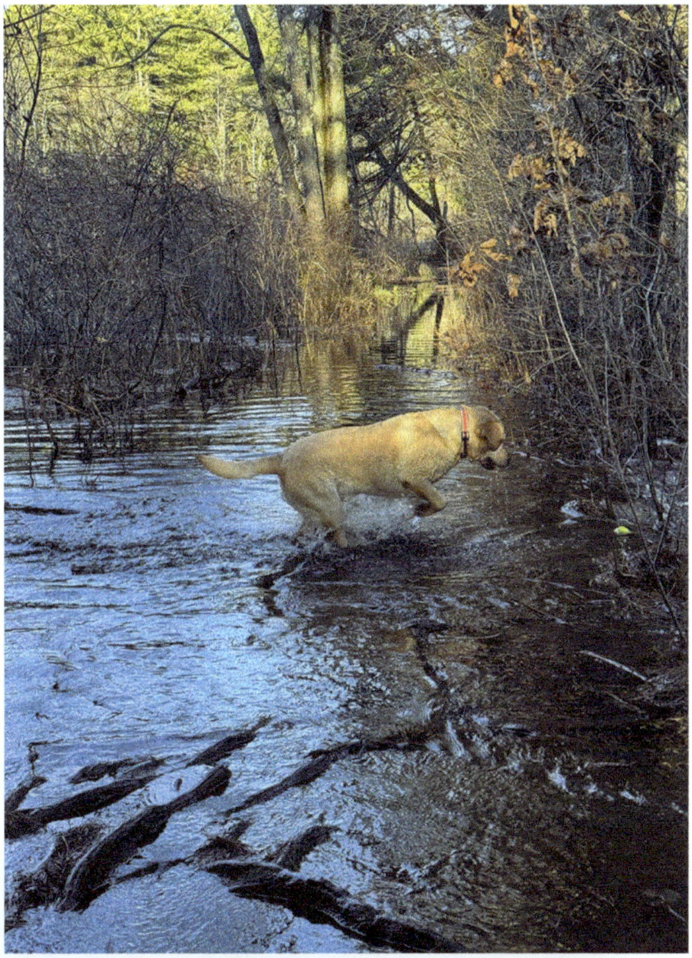

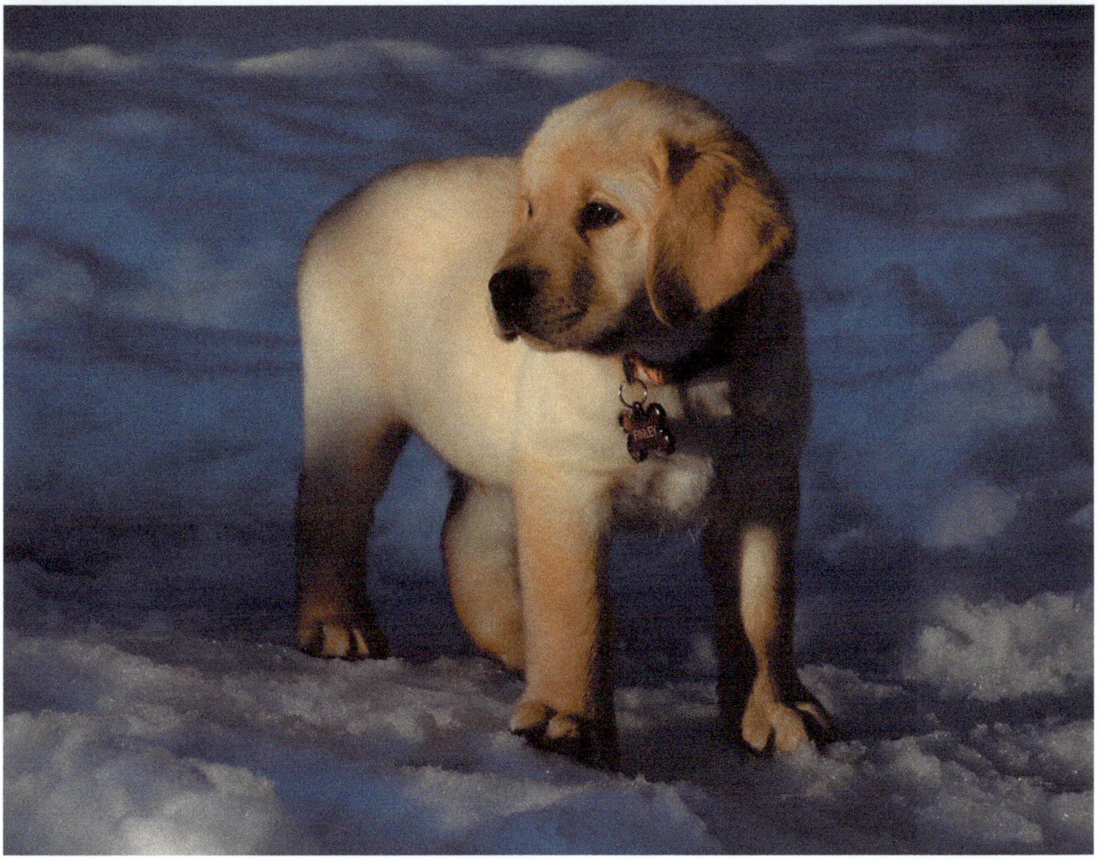

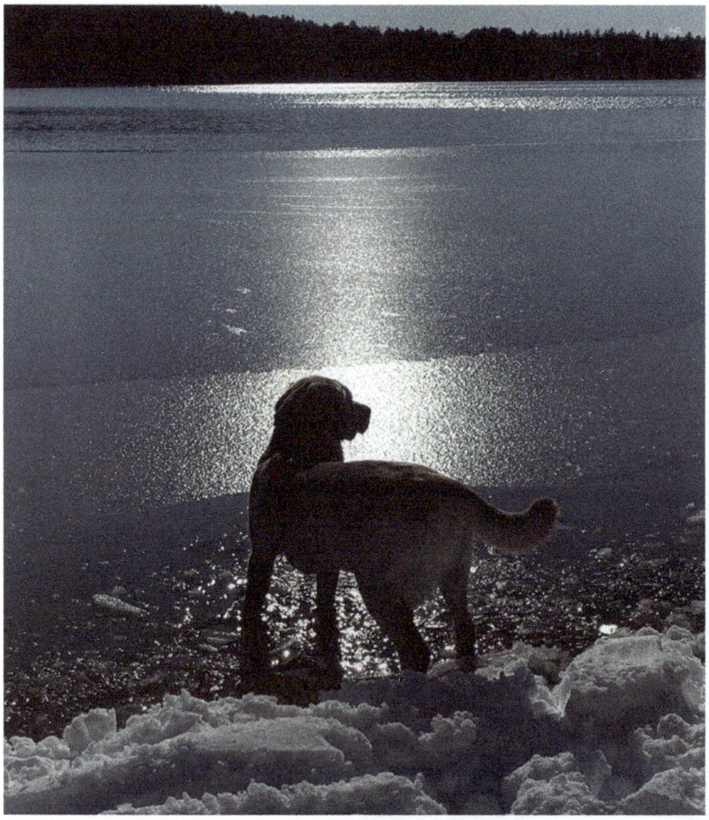
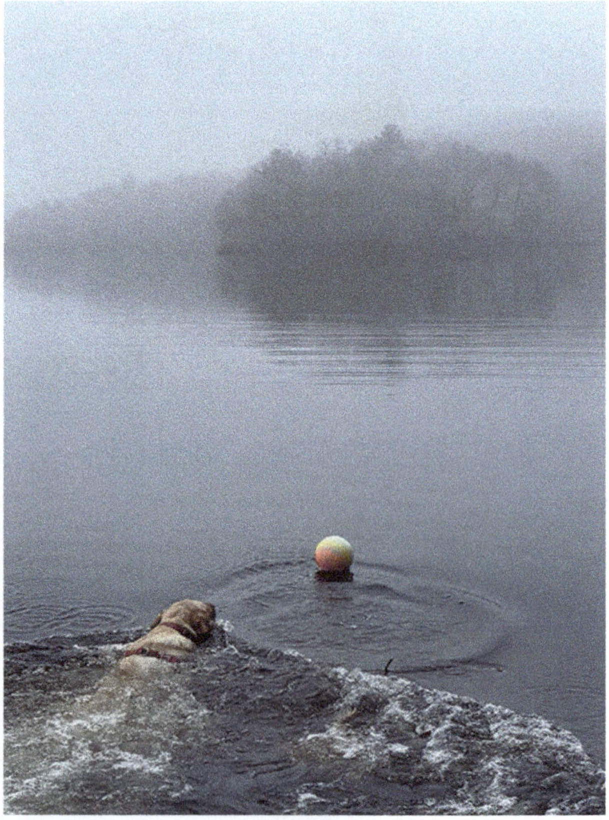
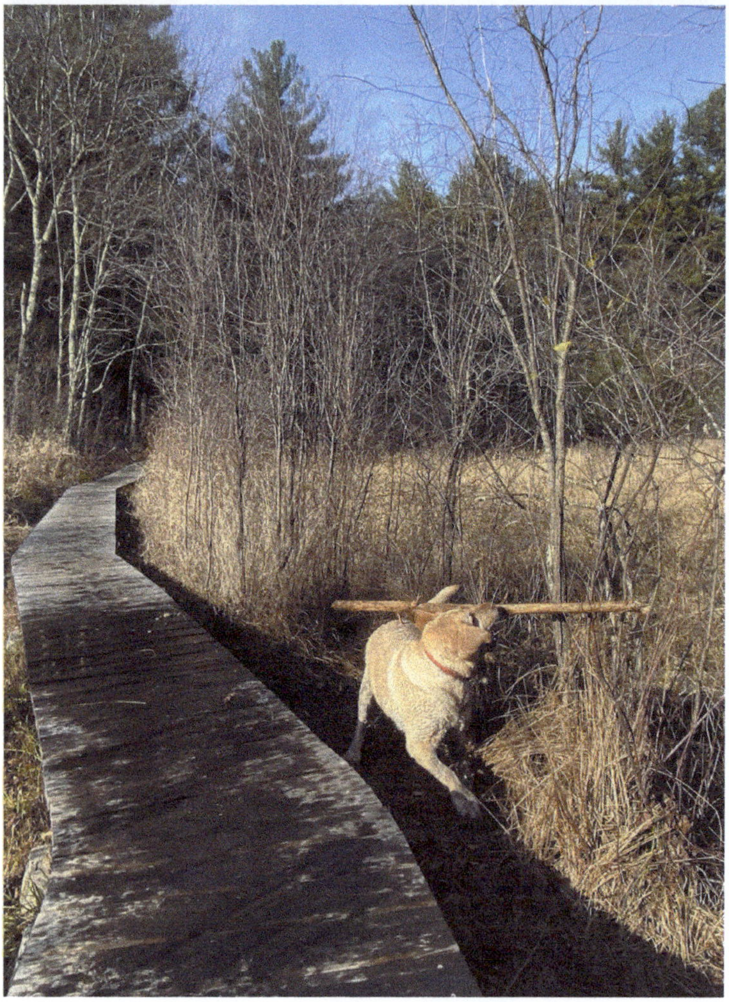

204

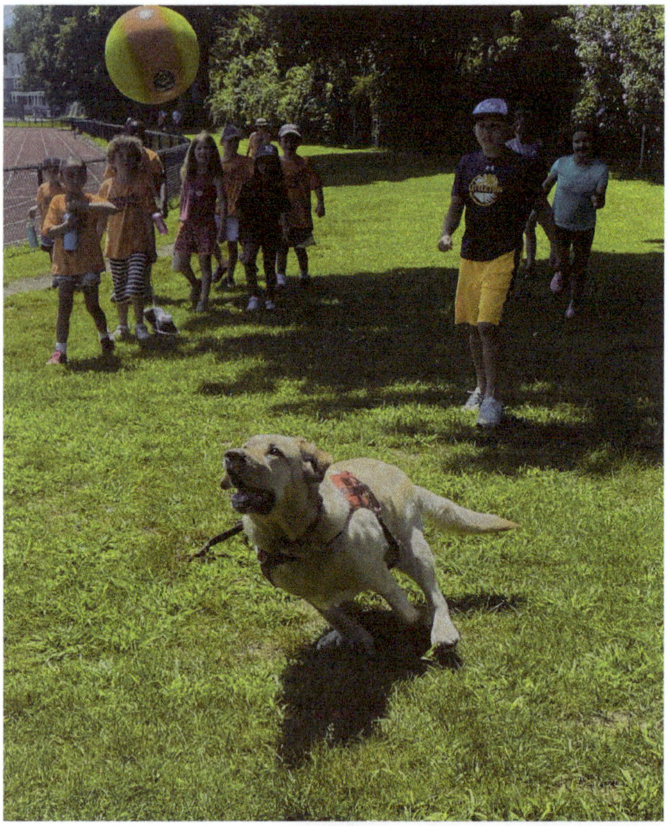

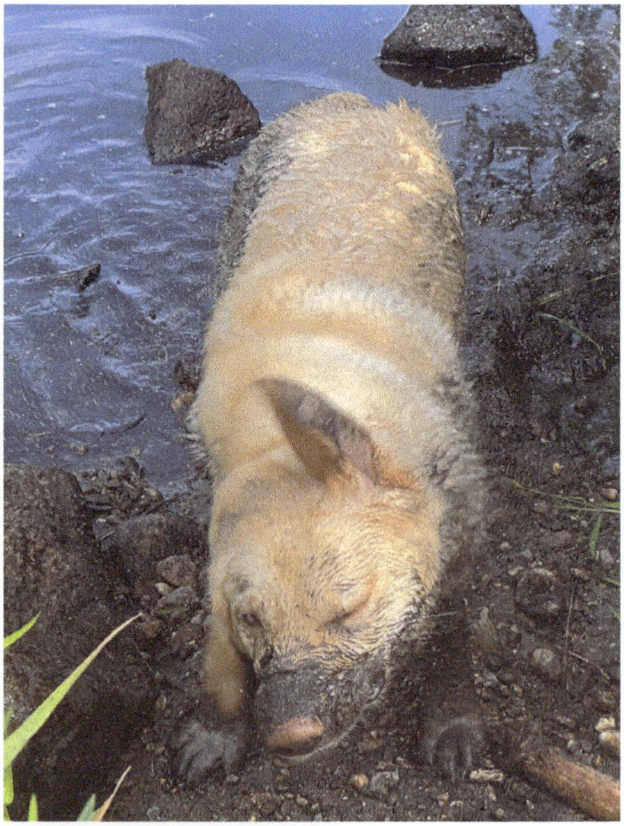

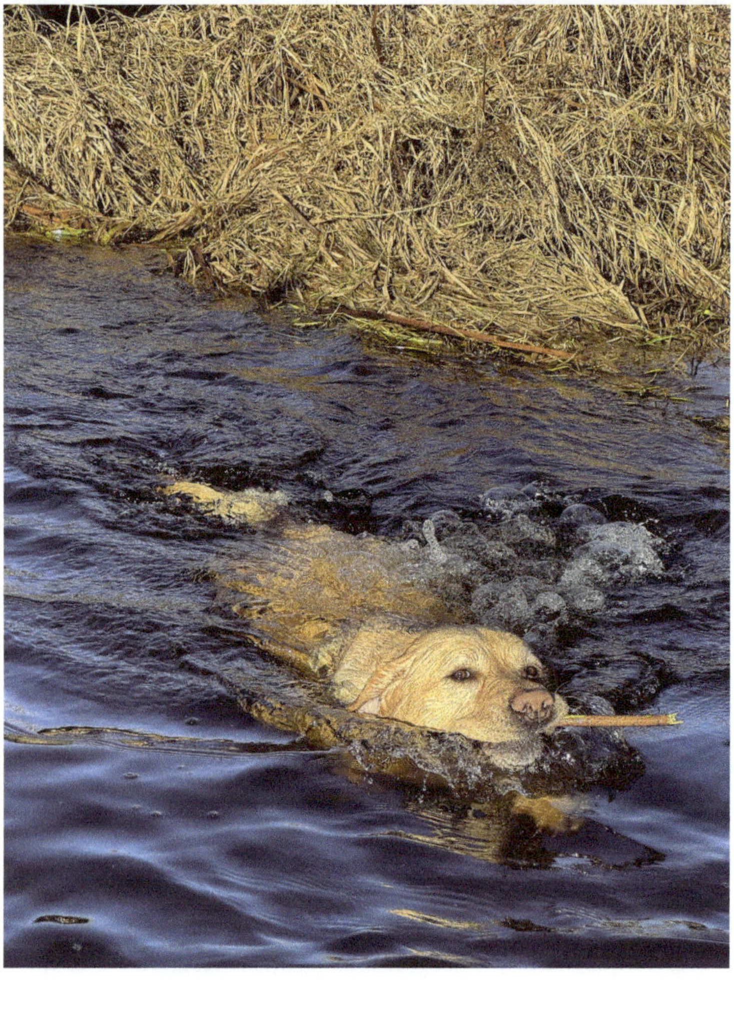

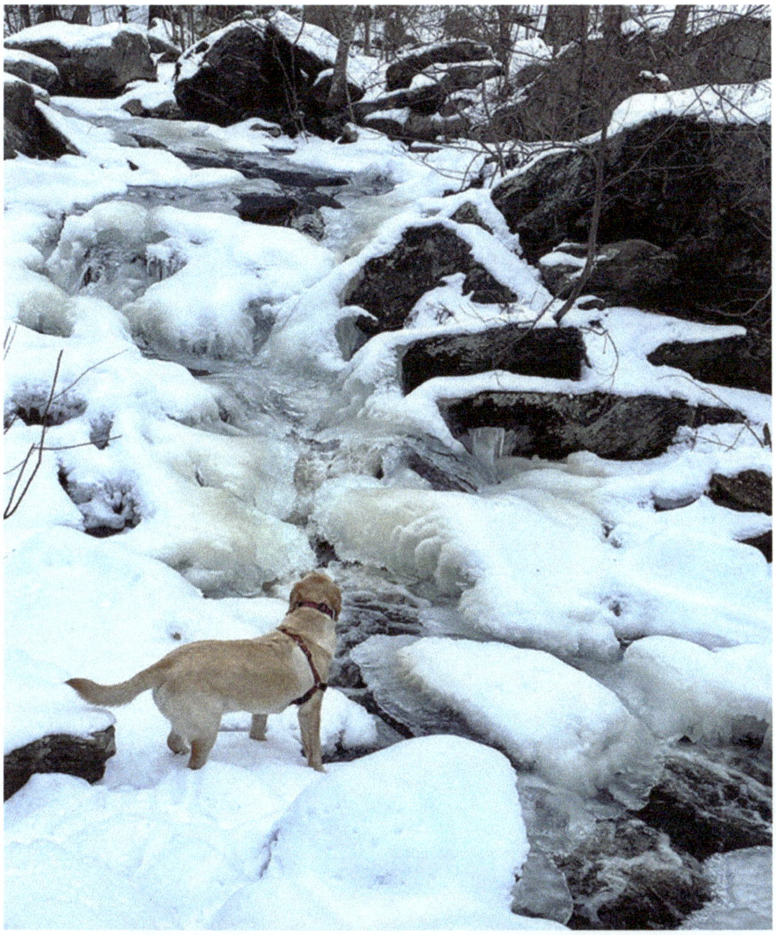
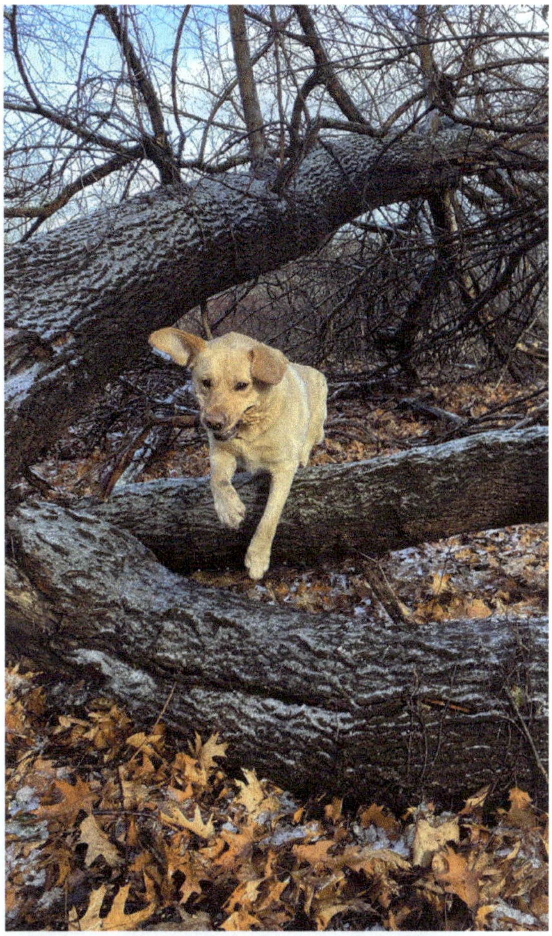
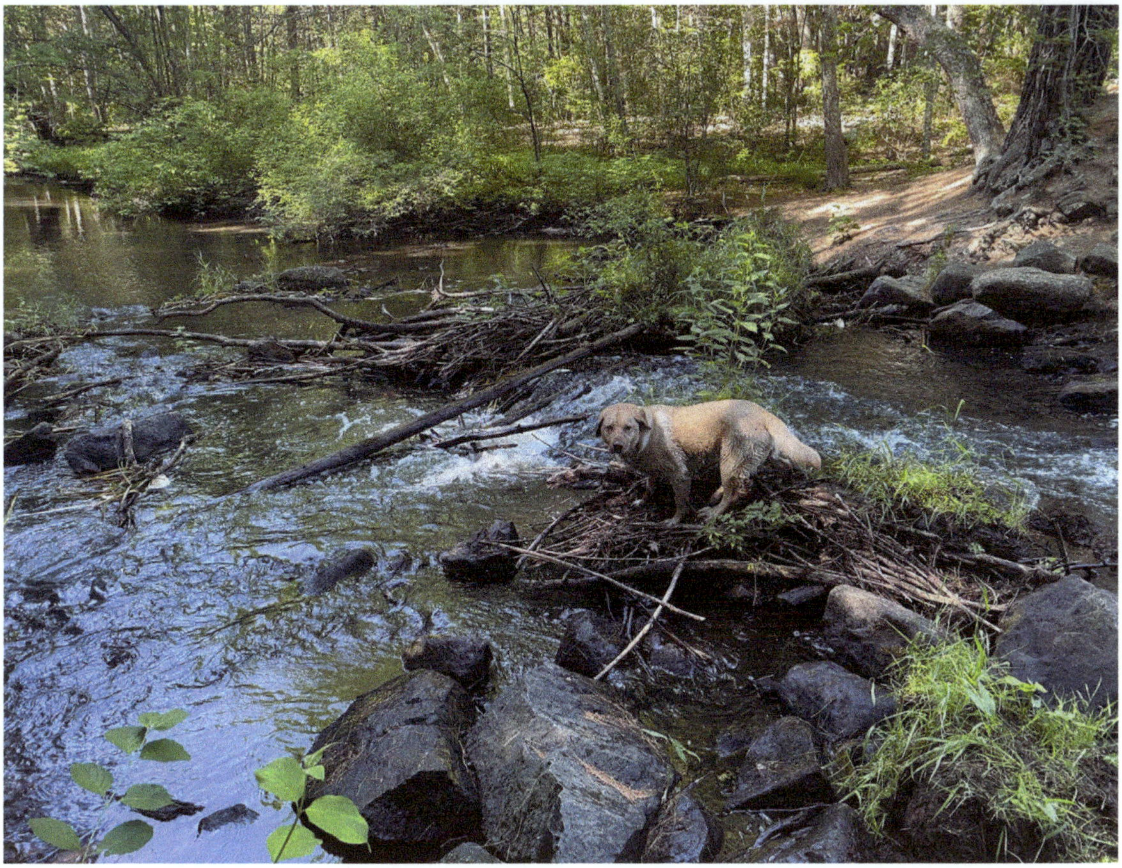

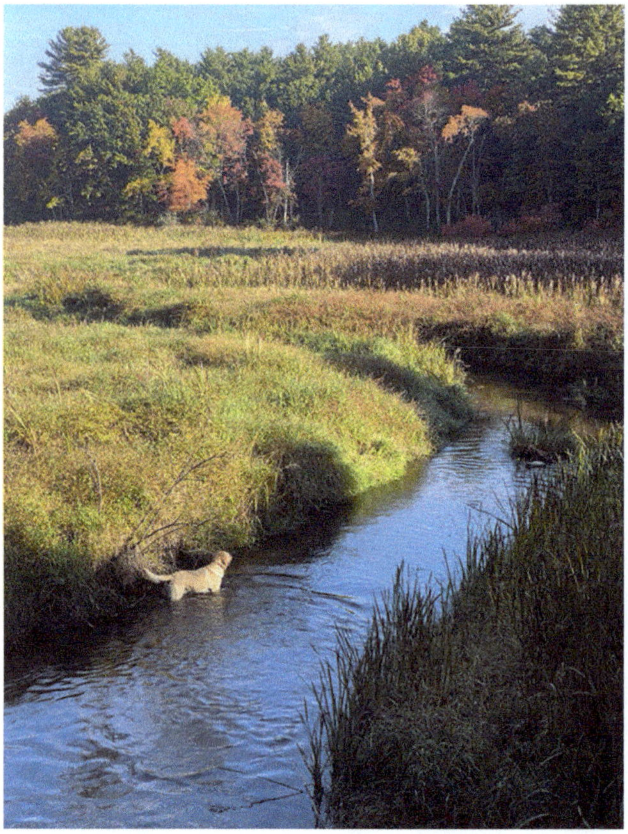

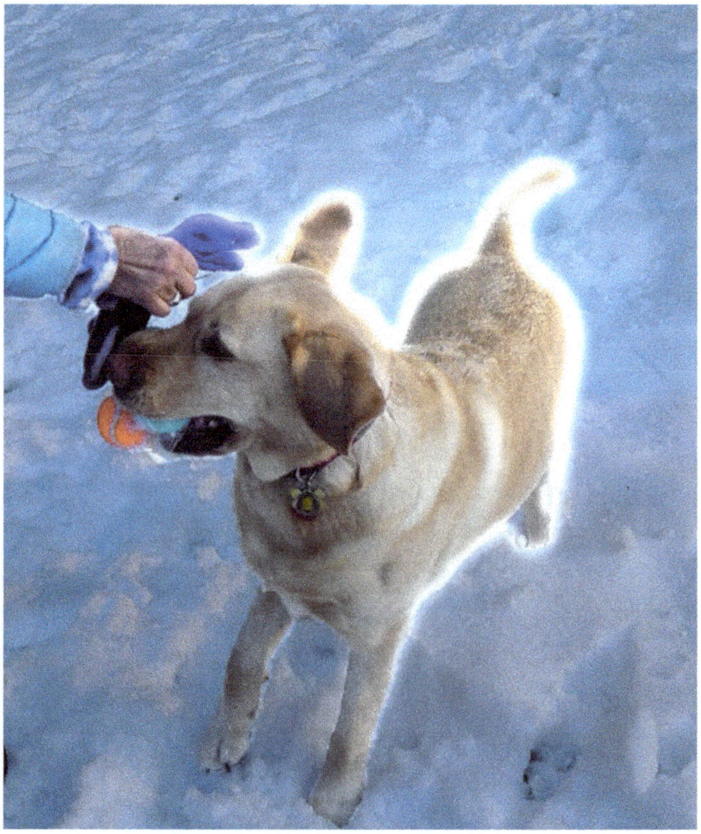

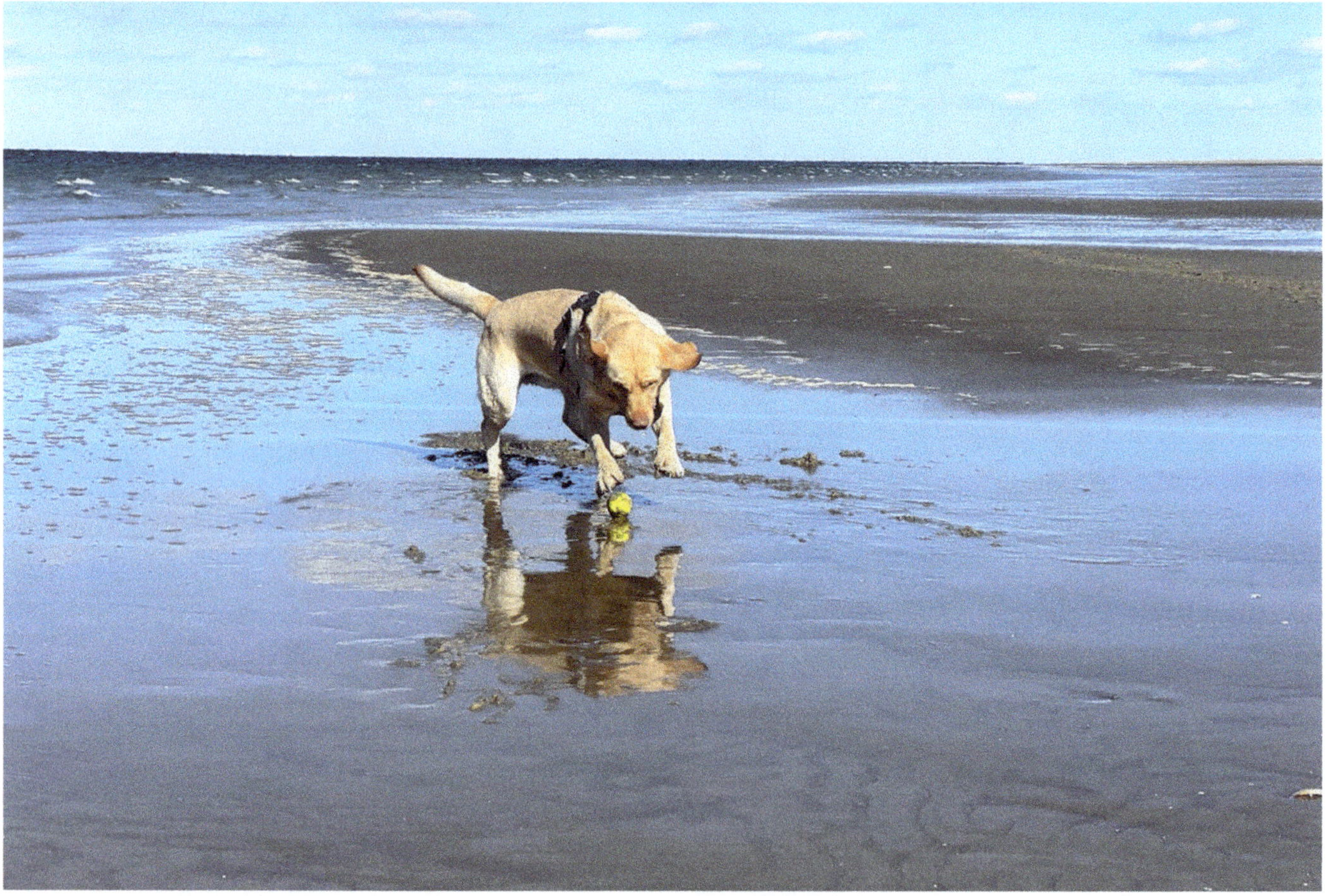

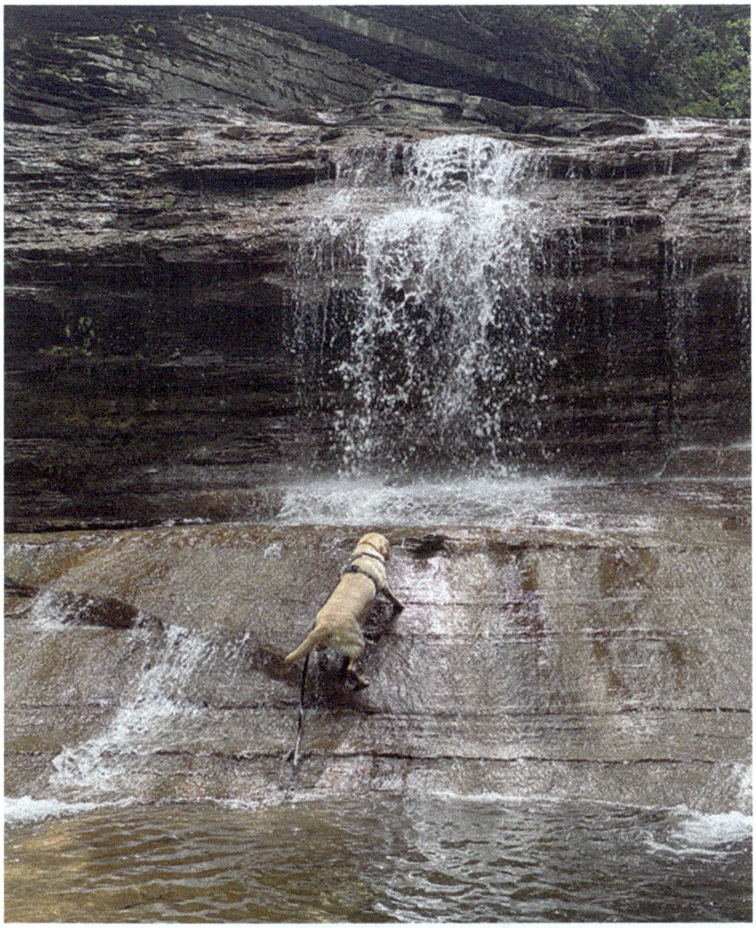

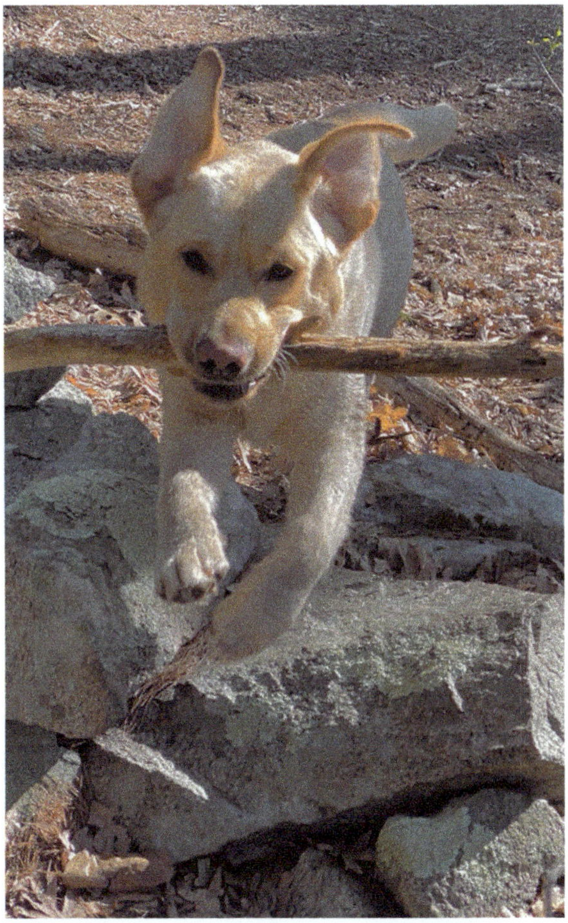

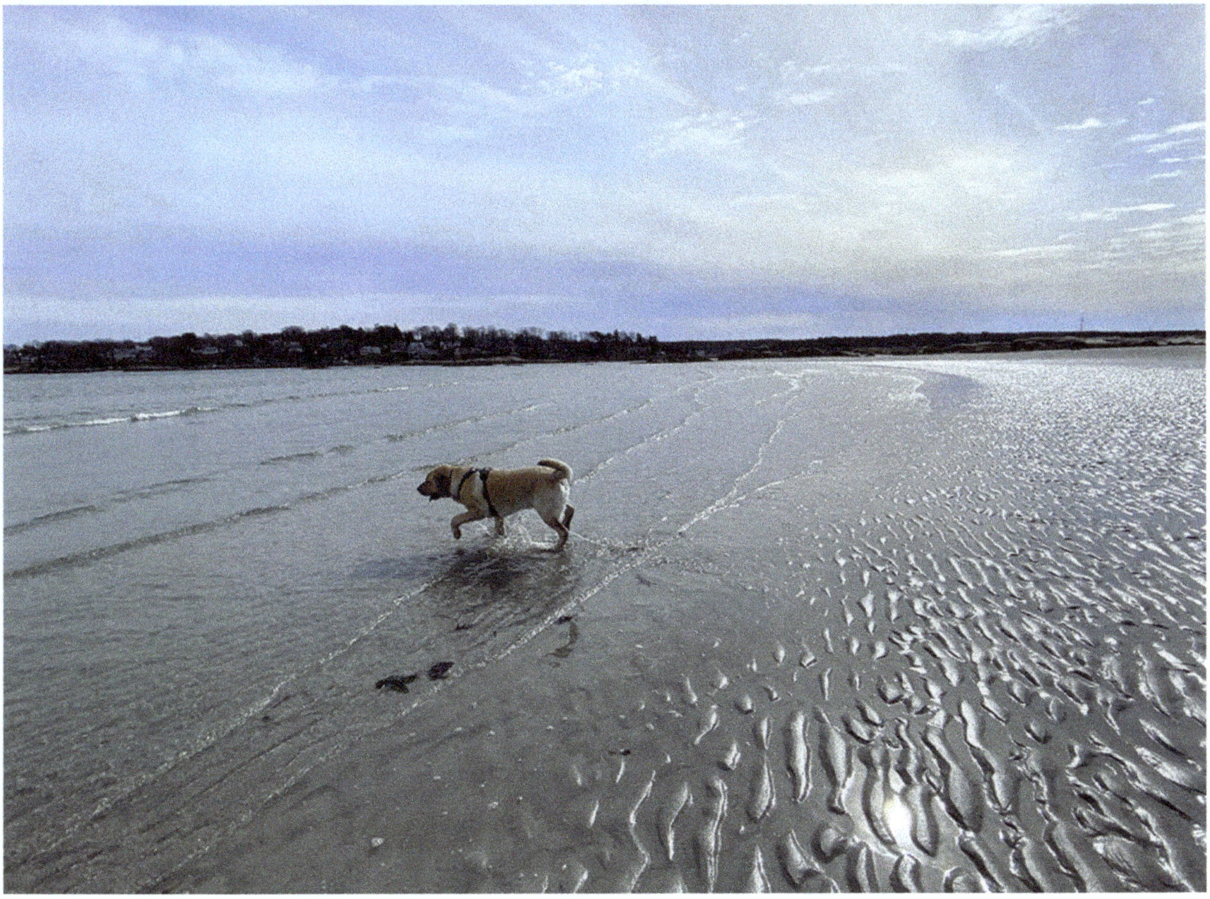

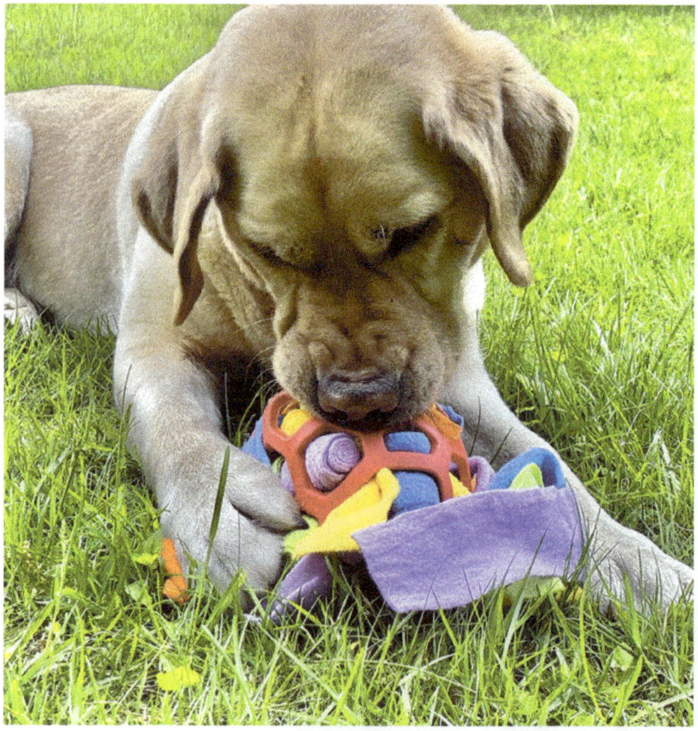

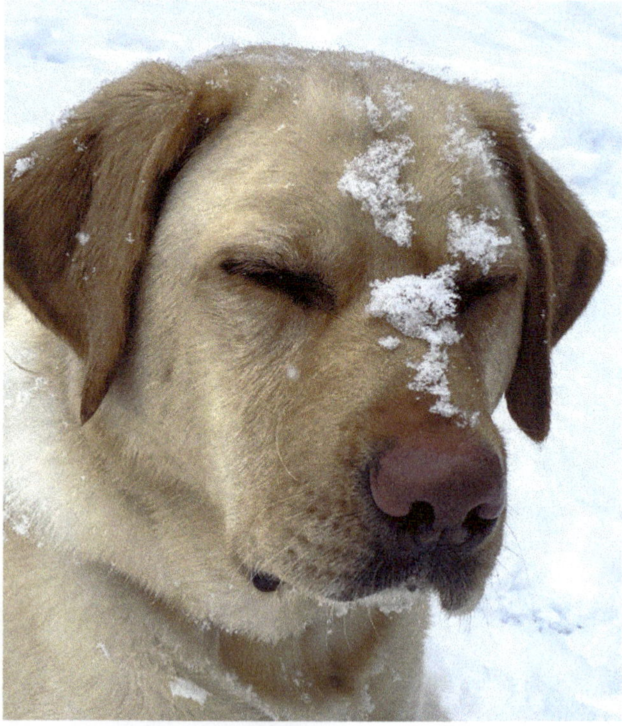

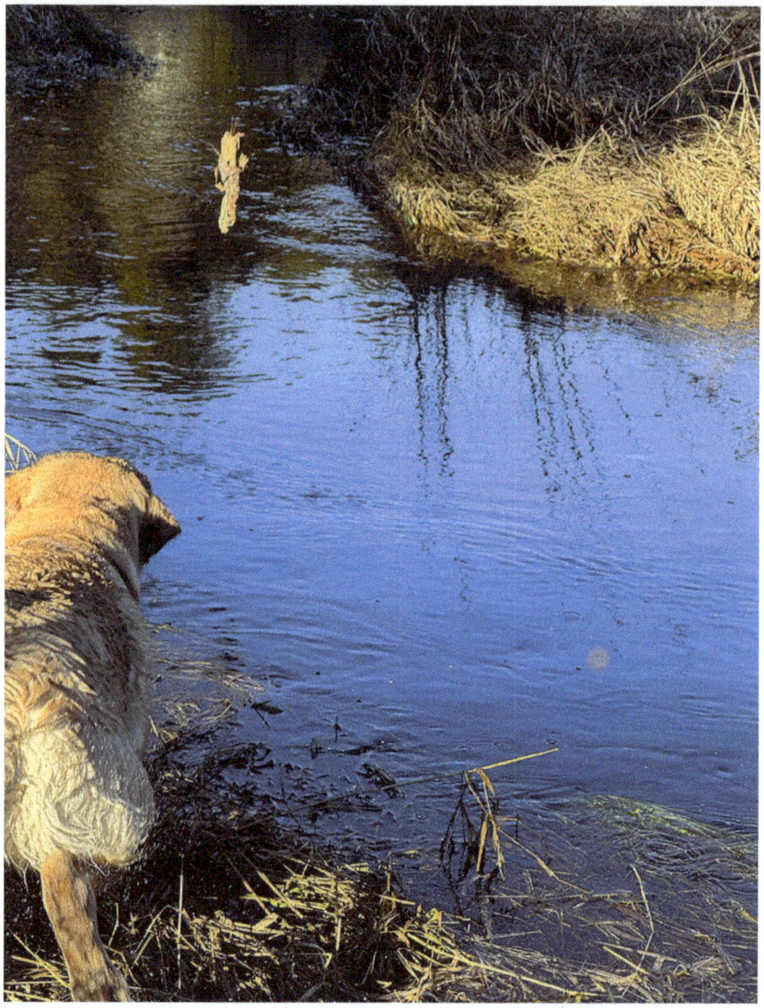

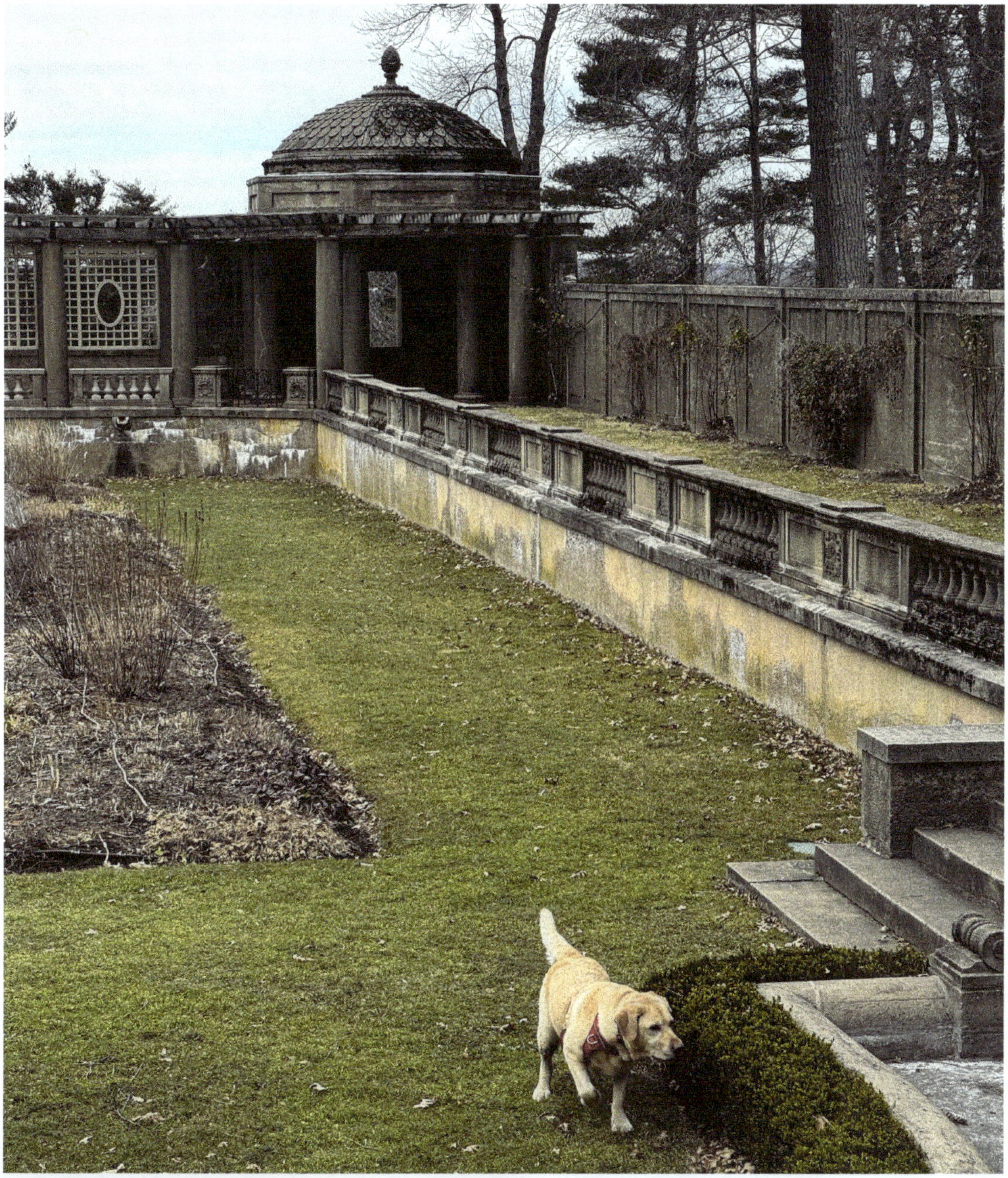

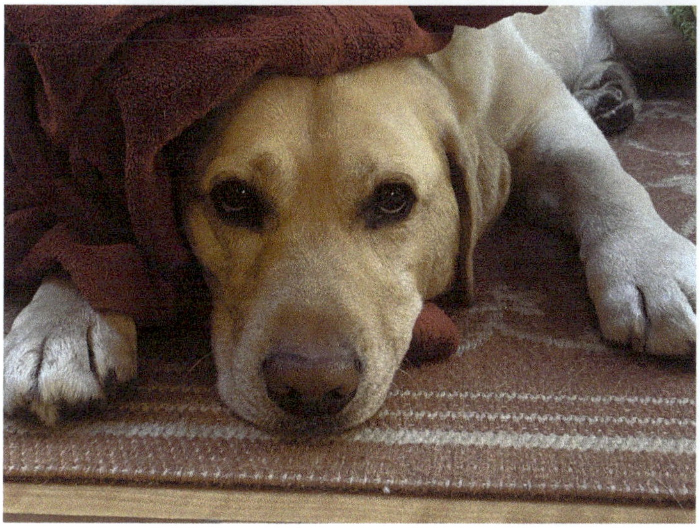

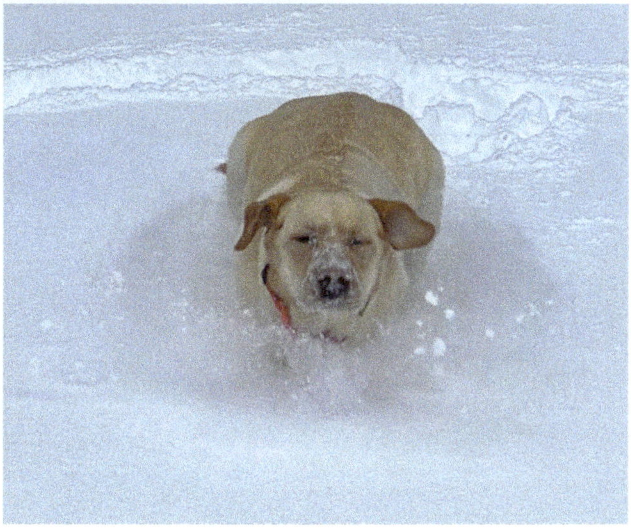

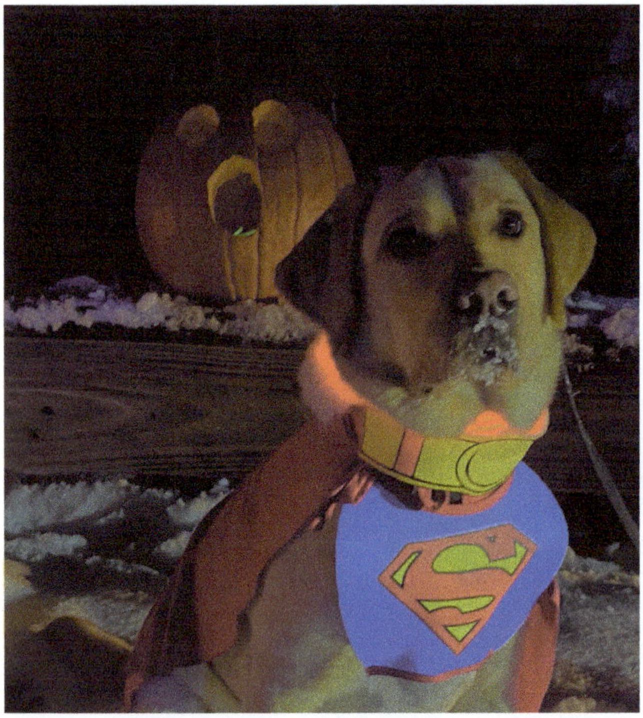
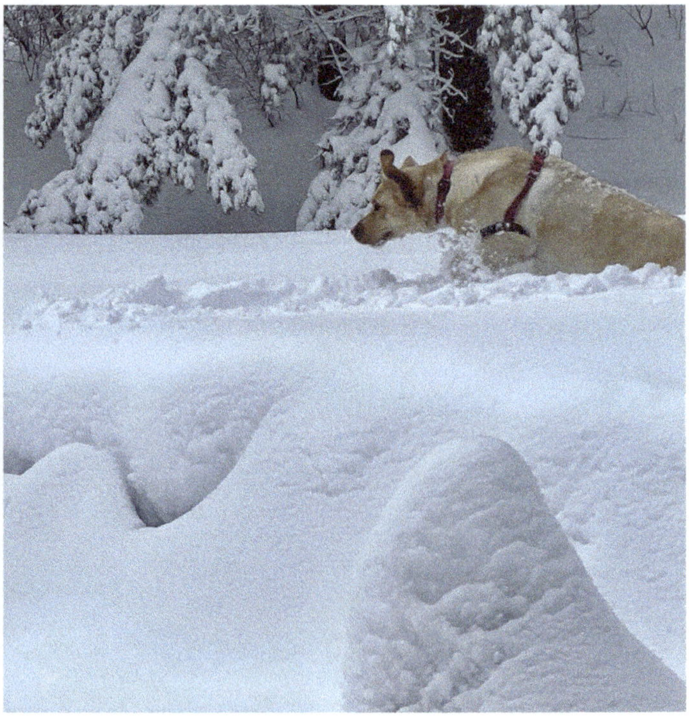
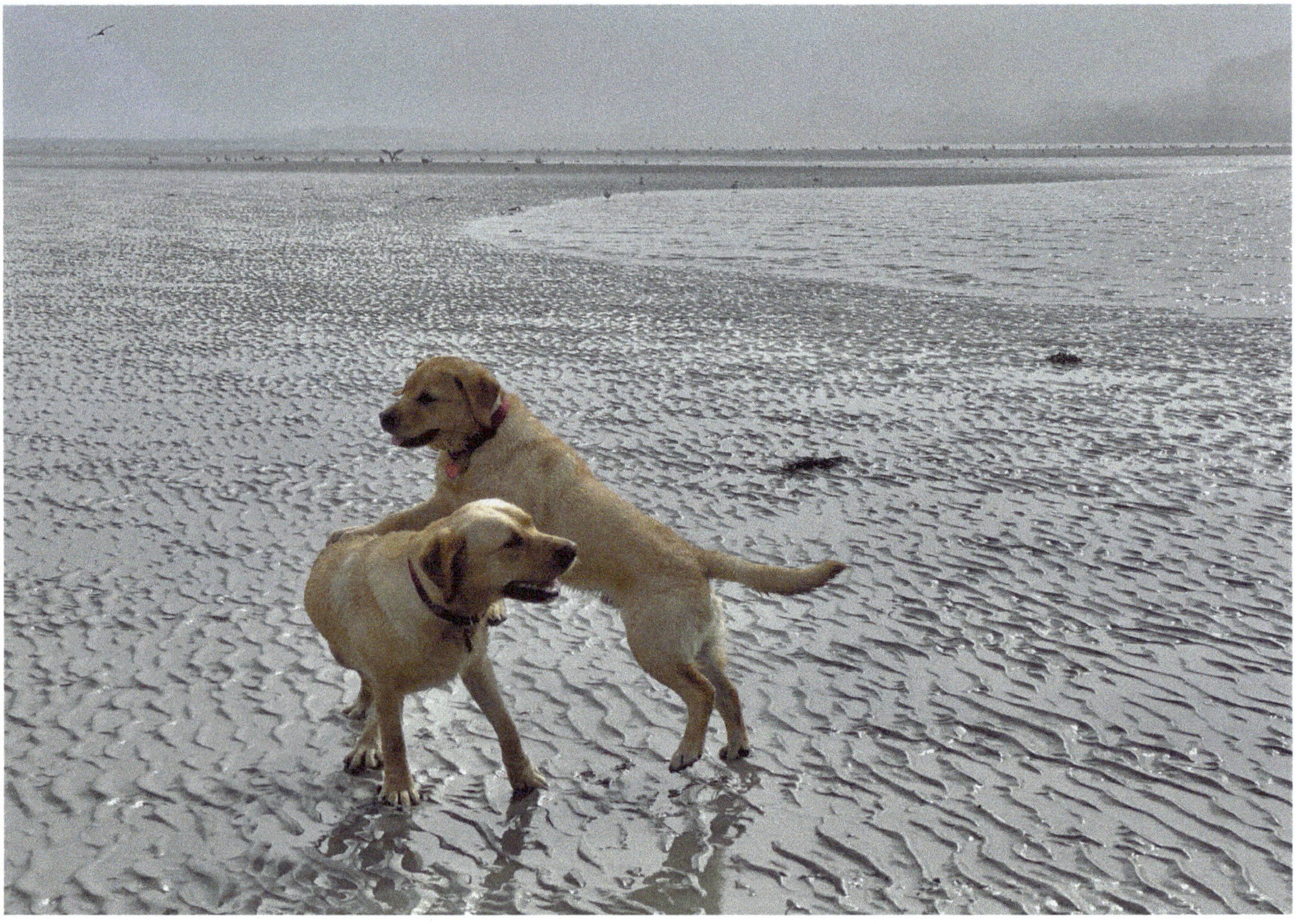

212

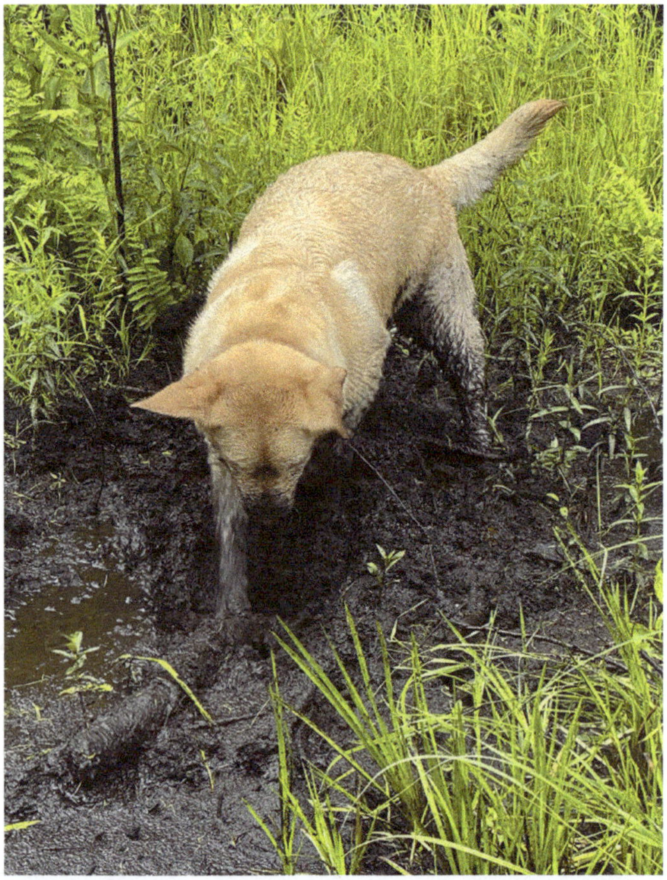

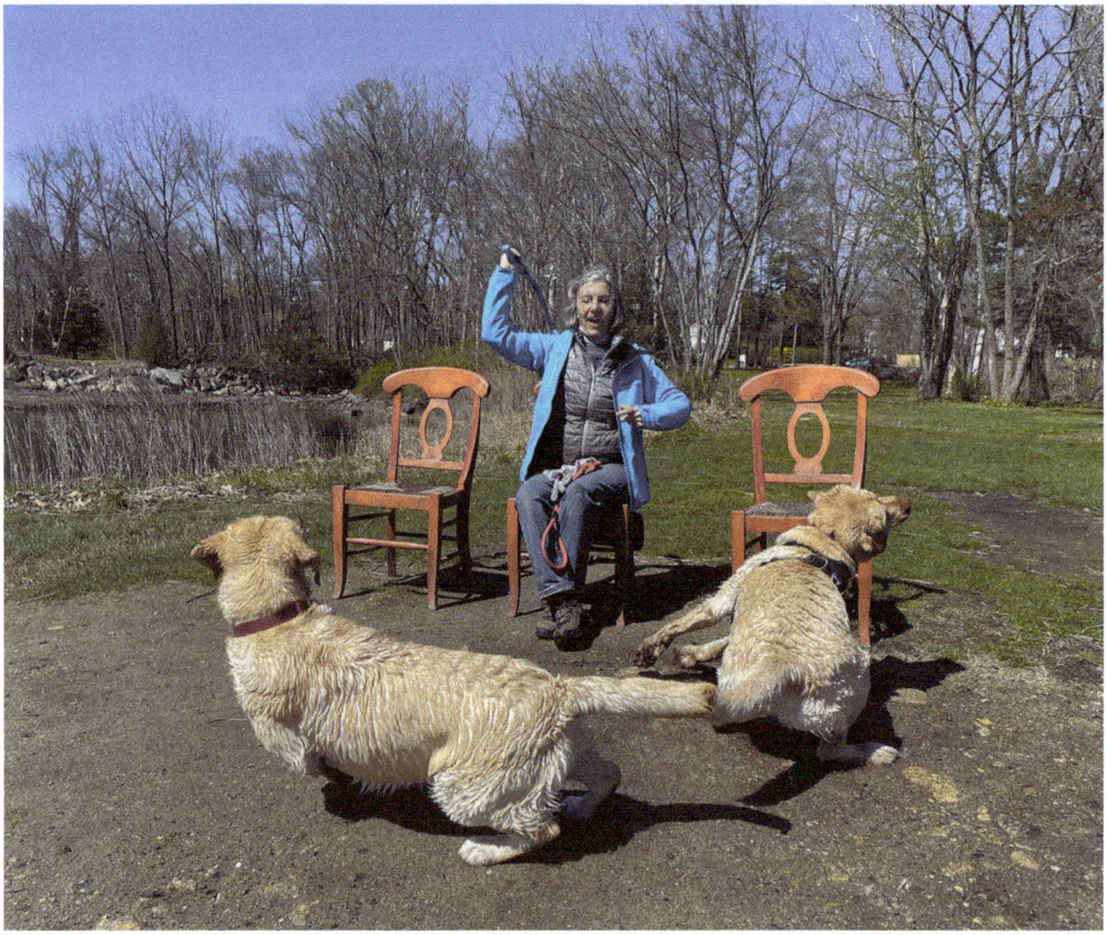

214

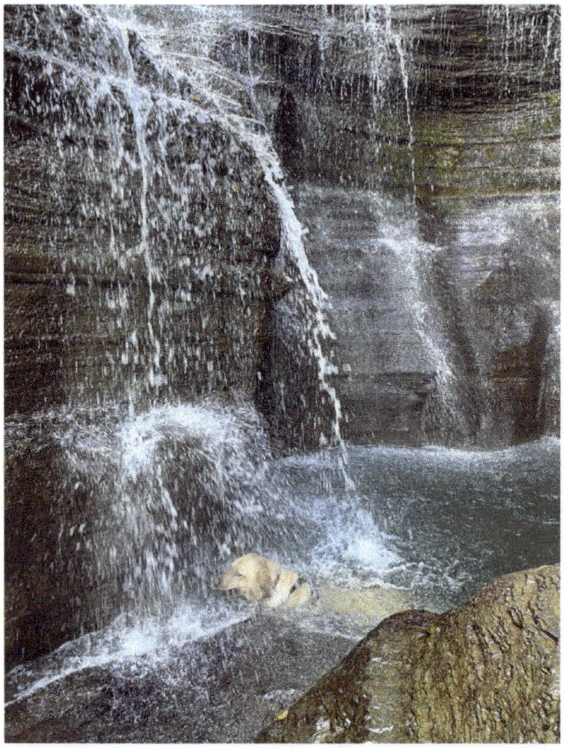

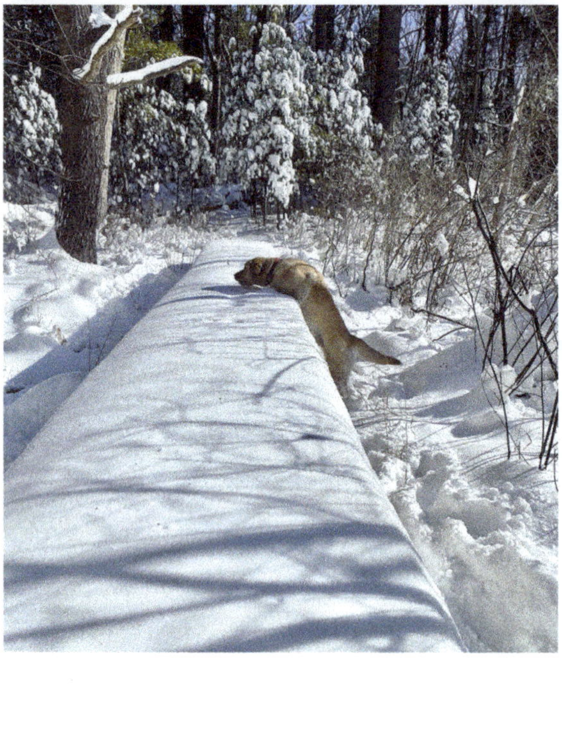

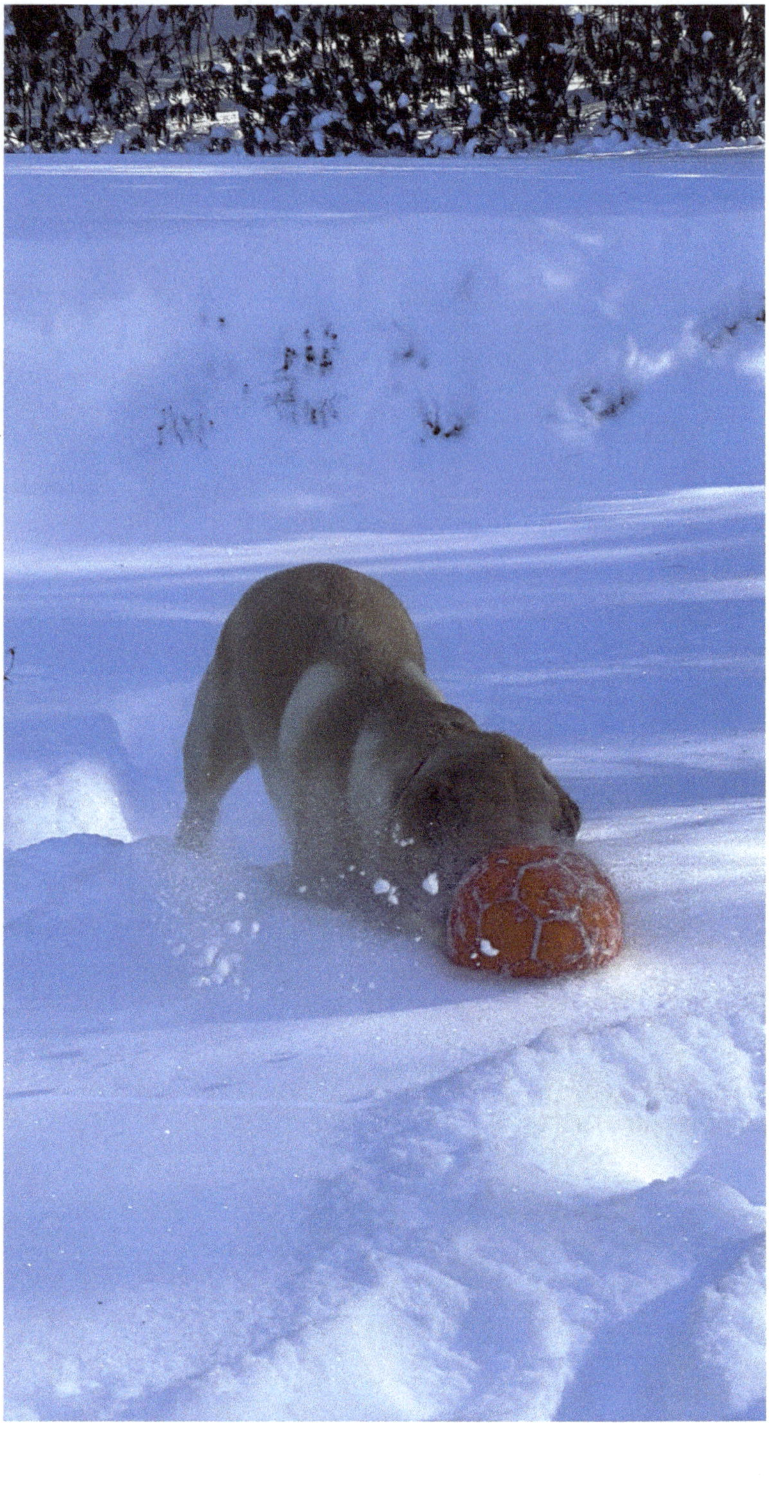

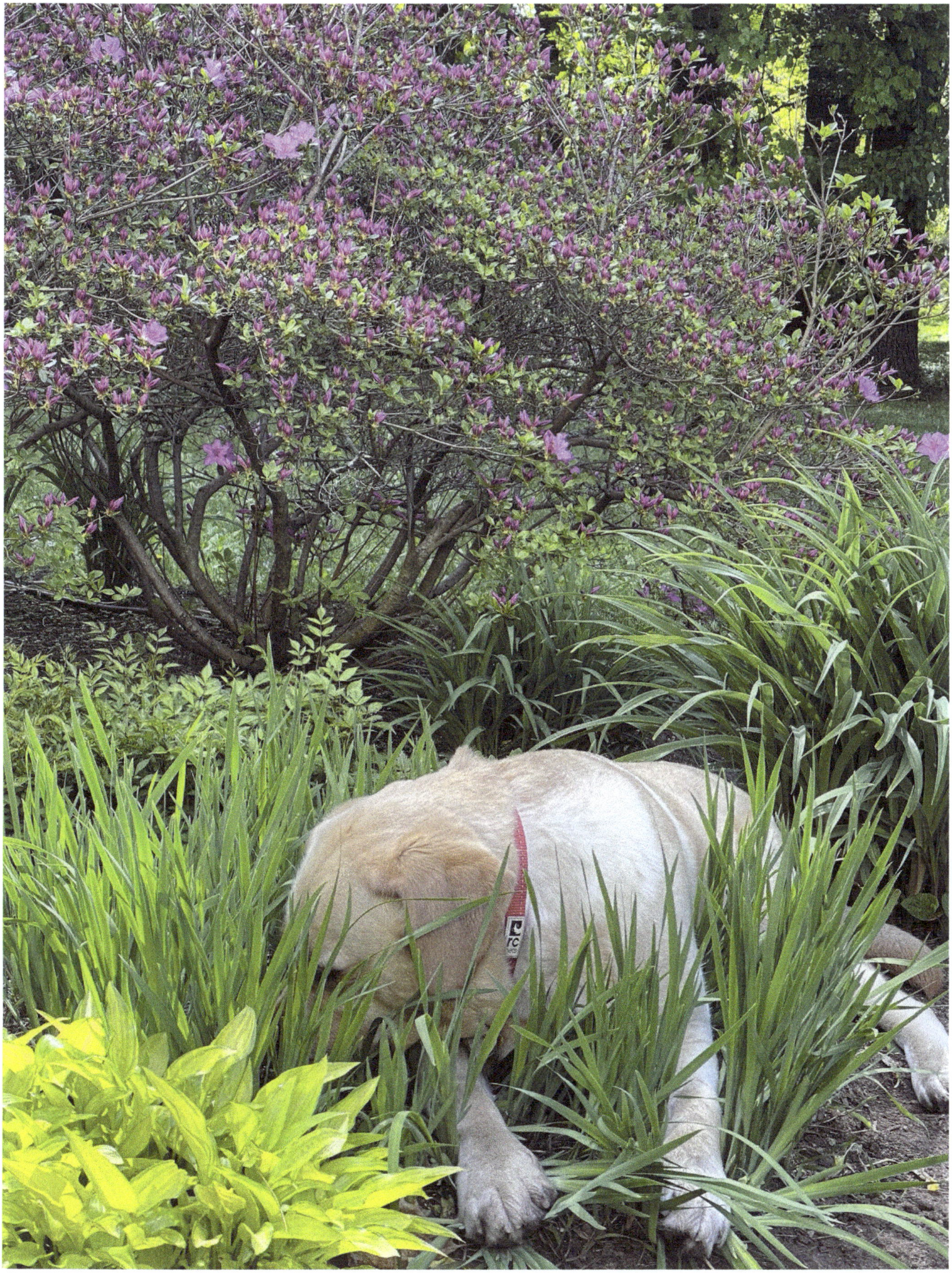

EPILOGUE

Dear readers,

Finley will be celebrating his 5th birthday on January 14, 2024. He continues to remain a puppy, though unofficially, in all aspects of his life. It is a distinct possibility that he will remain so for years to come.

As the sun sets on another beautiful bright autumn day here in southern New England, I am mindful of the coming cold. The date, February 4th, 2023, will be forever etched in my memory. At 7am, Finley rushed out the front door into an arctic blast with a windchill reading of minus 24 degrees, a record for our town. Finley didn't mind. In fact, he ran and retrieved sticks with such fervor that his paws never got cold enough to hinder him. Keeping my eyes on him throughout our walk, I thought of buying a couple of pairs of fleece-lined winter boots for extra protection for his very large paws.

Peace and love,
Sherry and Finley

ABOUT THE AUTHOR

Sherry Fendell lives in Sudbury, Massachusetts and is a professional photographer and world traveler. She has raised yellow Labrador Retrievers for thirty-five years, either from the young puppy stage of development or by rescuing older Labs who were given up for adoption. She has volunteered for Labrador Retriever Rescue for three years.

Finley's Adventures, published in weekly installments in the Sudbury Town Crier, became the most popular column between May of 2020 through May of 2022. Finley was often recognized by local residents in the woods of the town; both children and adults stopped to pet and/or hug him, usually telling Sherry how reading his stories brightened their day. They looked forward to reading the next installment of the Adventures. Many people spoke of learning about new places to explore with their own dog.

Sherry spoke of how it was always a great pleasure to meet Finley's admirers. Finley took in the laughter and love and would glow in the light of it.